WORK LESS
AND
PLAY MORE

Steven Catlin

KIMBERLITE PUBLISHING
Ventura, California

I

Cover design by Lightbourne Images © 1997
Illustrations by Leo Chiantelli

Library of Congress Cataloging-in-Publication Data
Catlin, Steven A., 1957–
    Work less and play more / Steven A. Catlin
        p.   cm.
    Originally published: Santa Barbara, Calif.: Fithian Press, 1989.
    Includes index.
    ISBN 0-9654188-0-4 (pbk.)
    1. Finance, Personal.   2. Time management.   I. Title
    HG179.C38   1997
    640'.43—dc21   96-50307
                                                                    CIP

Kimberlite Publishing
P.O. Box 6334
Ventura, California 93006

Printed on acid-free paper.
Printed in the United States of America.

*"The mass of men lead lives
of quiet desperation."*

HENRY DAVID THOREAU
(1817–1862)

Acknowledgements

Due to expansive gaps in my personal knowledge and skills, I was obliged to enlist the help of a number of persons in bringing this book to its final form. Thanks go to: Gary Catlin, Dave Stoeck, and Dan Francis for ideas; Fred and Patty Haynes for edits; Ramón Stevens for copy edits, page layout, and publishing advice; Leo Chiantelli for cartoons; Shannon Bodie and Gaelyn Larrick at Lightbourne Images for cover design; and Daina Catlin for general boundless enthusiasm and support.

Contents

1. Overworked and Underplayed 1
2. Time is Money, and Vice Versa 11
3. Murphy's Law 17
4. Building a Personal Treasury 21
5. Achieving Early Retirement 29
6. Semiretirement and Other Time-Off Options 35
7. The Nightmare of Credit 43
8. Reducing Purchase Costs 49
9. The Good Guys: Need and Investment Purchases 57
10. The "Maybe" Guys: Pleasure and Convenience Purchases 67
11. The Bad Guys: Ego, Tradition, and Guilt Purchases . . . 75
12. Avoiding Consequence Costs 83
13. Skipping the American Dream 89
14. The Value of Renting 95
15. Terminating Time Thievery 101
16. The Value of Organizing 105
17. The Law of Possessions 111
18. The Ultimate Possession: The House 121
19. Simplicity in the Extreme: Minimalism 131
20. Minimalism and the Cost of Living 137
21. Minimalism and Tax Laws 143
22. Achieving the Leisure Life 149
23. There is an Enemy 155
24. The Manipulators I: Madison Avenue 157
25. The Manipulators II: Salesmen 165
26. The Manipulators III: Employers 173
27. The Manipulators IV: The Government 181
28. The Old Man at the Campground 185
    Index 189

1

Overworked and Underplayed

On Saturday, October 10, 1992, Herbert Balfour Milhous of Sioux City, Iowa, stepped through the front doors of the Gold Mountain Casino in Las Vegas, Nevada. Looming in front of him was a colossal, seven-reel, one-dollar slot machine tied to a progressive jackpot. On his third try, Herbert lined up seven red "7" symbols and won $2.8 million. On Monday, October 12, Herbert Balfour Milhous turned in his notice at work, in the form of a full moon aimed at his beloved boss.

What an uplifting story! Oppressed employees everywhere should realize Herbert's fate. Bosses everywhere should suffer Herbert's boss's fate. Unfortunately, Herbert was lucky as hell. If you or I had pulled that handle, we'd have gotten two plums, a bell, and four lemons. We're as likely to win

Herbert Milhous gives his notice

$2.8 million as to spend Saturday night with Claudia Schiffer (okay, Brad Pitt) or hop a ride on the next space shuttle.

I believe, however, that what Herbert did is readily achievable by most working people today. Not the part about lining up seven 7s, but delivering two weeks notice. (Though I'd have to wonder if Herbert's boss was willing to tolerate two more weeks of him.) If you earn even a modest income and can muster a scant half-teaspoon of discipline, you can say good-bye to your boss too.

Thank God It's Friday

Why is Monday "Blue" and Friday "Thank God it's..."? Who invented work, anyway? Dogs don't do it. Fish don't do it. They're getting along fine. Let's all pile in a time machine and go back and pound the guy who invented the plow.

As I see it, the two great offenses of work are:

1. Work thieves your time.
2. Work stresses you out.

No wonder some people prefer to skip working and instead live in a cardboard box; work prevents you from doing the things you enjoy, and provides as a replacement a sort of lifelong, body-destroying torture. Where's that time machine?

Let's look at an example of Offense No. 1, time thievery. It's the story of "Bo" Parsons, an employee of Shackles Oil Company, where yours truly worked during the mid 1980s.

I never actually met Bo. I read of him in the company newsletter. Twice. The first piece on Bo described his retirement party. Bo had worked an amazing 37 years for Shackles Oil. The article listed his work achievements, provided pictures of Bo with co-workers and Shackles' management, and supplied a few quotes on Bo's retirement plans. Oh, yes, Bo received the gold watch.

Sadly, the next bit on Bo was his obituary. He had died just one month after retiring. Obviously, he'd enjoyed only trifling amounts of fishing, golfing, and visiting his grandchildren in that time.

In a sense, Shackles had stolen Bo's life. They had used him up and sent him away on "E." But, too, Bo had let it happen. We must conclude he either truly loved his work (huh?), or he wasn't aware he had any other options.

Bo may have thrived at Shackles, but I found it a stressful place to work. It seemed to me an environment where politics counted more than productivity, and upper management was adverse. Also, vacation time was minimal. I would have stepped off a high bridge before spending 37 years there.

Evidence of Offense No. 2, stress, is ubiquitous: Post Office employees routinely crack like eggs, L.A. drivers take shots at each other, and women who have entered the workplace now drop from heart attacks as often as men. There are ulcers galore, and drinking problems, and pill problems. People can't sleep at night. Many individuals try desperately to vent the stress in healthy ways: they run, bike, or lift weights. They try to escape it all by hiking deep into the mountains.

Wouldn't it be nice to skip the stress in the first place? To live the dog's life; to be that turtle on the log in the sun? How about taking half of those 40 to 50 years of productive adulthood and using them to your own ends: traveling, reading, hiking, skiing, playing a musical instrument, painting pictures, spending time with your friends and family. It's possible. Don't be a Bo.

Door Number One, Two, or Three

The ideas set forth in this book constitute a sweeping plan of life simplification, with the gratifying end result of a huge increase in leisure time. It is possible to fully embrace the plan or, alternatively, to pick and choose from its separate points to still reap a significant partial benefit. Depending on the degree to which you implement the plan, as well as on factors unique to your life, you can choose from three time-off options:

The Ultimate — Early Retirement
The Exciting — Semiretirement
The Still Pretty Darn Pleasing — Increased vacation, multiple leaves without pay

The individual life factors most likely to influence the degree of leisure you can personally achieve are your income level and the number of unshakable responsibilities you carry (the biggest of these will probably be any children you have under age 18). As we proceed, we will look at examples of people who have achieved each of these immensely rewarding goals.

The Four Cornerstones

It is possible to substantially increase your leisure time, or even cast off the work yoke entirely, without giving up anything truly vital to your happiness. I maintain this opinion because I truly believe that people today generate their own life complexity through the choices they make. Despite what in fact may be the greatest opportunity yet in American history to live simply and comfortably with a minimum of effort, the general populace persists in helping themselves to more than they need (usually on credit), then choking on the excess. I believe they do this because they have been badgered and brainwashed by tradition, Madison Avenue, their bosses, and the government.

The *Work Less and Play More* plan primarily involves changing attitudes. A major life restructuring can be achieved essentially by coming to certain realizations, rather than by making great sacrifices. (Who would want a book that tells you to sacrifice?)

The Four Cornerstones of the strategy are:

1. minimize possessions
2. accept no hangers-on (i.e., dependents)
3. don't own a house
4. defend against those who covet your time and money

Most everyone is in a position to accomplish Items 1 and 4, minimizing possessions and warding off those who want to grab a piece of you. And considerable life simplification will result if you do accomplish these. Everyone should give Item 3 their strong consideration. A house purchase can be a tremendous blunder. A personally owned home can be a ball and chain. Item 2 concerns a rather emotion-charged issue. People will generally follow their hearts on this issue, but please do consider the arguments offered (Chapter 13).

Work Less and Play More is a book for mainstream America of the late 20th century. It advocates casting off the widespread practice of materialism that arose on a broad scale in the post-World War II era and culminated with the Yuppie experience of the early 1980s. The book's antimaterialism message is based upon the doctrine of rational selfishness (as set forth in the writings of Ayn Rand) in combination with sound reasoning, rather than upon moral or purely philosophical grounds. It is by no means offered as a counter-cultural message.

The Famous Visit to the Closet

Allow me to relate a bit of my own story at this juncture. It should supply you with an understanding of my slant on this whole subject, and provide an example of a conversion: a hardworking, would-be ladder-climber transformed into a leisure-embracing minimalist. I call my moment of dawning realization "The Famous Visit to the Closet."

It was 1984 (no, this has nothing to do with George Orwell). I was four years out of college with a geology degree in hand, and was working at my second full-time job, for a company called Indentured International Oil. My first career try, in mining geology, had fallen by the wayside when I had concluded that summer-long, 70-hour-per-week work stints in places like Eureka, Utah, and Winnemucca, Nevada, were upsetting my delicate constitution. The new job was an improvement: saner hours, higher pay, human beings for company rather than Gila monsters and rattlesnakes. Indentured International was thriving; it appeared I had a promising future there. Following the advice and example of my peers, I bought a new car and a townhouse — on credit.

One evening I was digging in the closet for some old textbooks. The books were stashed in a box at the back, so to get at them I had to excavate a bunch of my toys. Tossing a tennis racket behind me, I thought, "Gee, Steve, you haven't played tennis in a while. You'll have to give Charlie a call." Next it was my fishing gear: "Damn, Roger told me about that great bass pond near his land, but I still haven't gone out there." Then it was my golf clubs: "I haven't been golfing in a year." (Probably because I shot a 120 the last time out, but let's forget that for the moment.) On and on it went. Finally, I stopped and looked around at all my forsaken playthings. I had hardly used any of them since getting out of school. All I had done was work, work, work. Mind you, I was an up-and-coming success story in the classic sense. I had all the things that were supposed to make me happy. But the real truth was that I had been happier as a lowly grad student. Something was wrong.

I began then to develop and place into action a plan of escape. I de-emphasized career success and put a stop to the pointless (actually, thoroughly detrimental) accumulation of status symbols and other material goods. I began saving money and, by doing that, slowly eliminated my dependence on continuous employment.

One final event drove home the lessons learned in The Famous Visit to the Closet. Just a month or so later, Indentured International was wiped out in a merger. Suddenly, I was faced with the prospect of having to make home and car payments without the benefit of a regular paycheck. I came to realize one more disadvantage of playing the Yuppie: you often get yourself out on a limb. I managed to save myself in this case by landing a job with another big oil company (Shackles), but I'd had a good scare. I wasn't going to make the same mistakes again.

On to the Leisure Life

And so I toiled away at Shackles Oil. It was a foul experience — the boss was a drunk, and the company poorly managed (overmanaged, actually: 14 layers between the lowest secretary and the CEO). But now there was light at the

8

end of the tunnel. I dumped the townhouse and paid off the car (a modest compact, or I would have traded down). Money started piling up in the bank.

Then disaster struck my workplace again. The oil glut had arrived. Layoffs began, and people at work started chewing their nails. That is, most of them did. This time I was ready.

Circumstances in the oil industry deteriorated and one day I was called in by the company's employee relations department. They gave me the option of taking "voluntary layoff" with generous severance pay. (I got the impression "involuntary layoff" was right around the corner if I would have said no.) I accepted, and went home and celebrated. It was spring, and I decided to take the entire summer off before even considering working again.

That summer was four-and-a-half months of purest bliss. In early May I threw a tent and sleeping bag into the trunk of my car, put everything else I owned in a storage locker, and hit the back roads. I didn't return until mid-September. In between, I traveled through 31 states and five Canadian provinces. I visited friends and family, toured museums, and viewed the splendors of over a dozen national parks. Along the way I hiked, fished, spotted wildlife, gazed at the stars, and devoured stacks of books. The strains of the work world were forgotten. The accumulated tension melted out of my body.

Occasionally on the journey, I would find myself involved in a discussion about my Man of Leisure status. The usual response from individuals hearing of my time off and of my travel plans was something like, "You're so lucky," or "I wish I could join you." It was as if my break had been made possible by some massive stroke of luck; a lottery win, say, or sudden inheritance. In fact, I spent about $900 per month that summer. My Shackles Oil severance had funded the entire excursion.

I was able to take such a lengthy break, at minimal cost, because I had reduced my possessions, disposed of the townhouse, and otherwise eliminated demands on my time and money. My life was in one sense simple, but paradoxically, was more fulfilling as a result.

You, too, can escape the clutches of work. May you be lounging in a hammock seaside this time next year!

2

Time is Money, and Vice Versa

The Value of Time and Money

Time is probably a person's most precious resource, though we typically don't realize it until we start to run out. Everything pleasurable in life requires time. We probably all wish we had more time, at least more free time (a longer visit to the dentist we could do without). When our time is wasted, we get annoyed. Traffic jams, trips to the store to return faulty merchandise, and perhaps those obligatory holiday visits to the in-laws all tick us off.

Money is a precious resource too. This may be unfortunate, but it is 20th-century reality. Money can get you most anything: a lobster dinner, a Hawaiian vacation, a new car. If you have enough of it, you can buy a baseball team, marry a Playboy Playmate, or make a run for president. Almost any problem can be solved with money: appliances can be repaired; noses can be fixed; if you're cold you can move to a place with nicer weather. There are exceptions — for example, health problems. But even in these situations, money helps. Money can buy the best medical care.

The availability of time and the availability of money are two of the greatest factors affecting your quality of life. There are other major factors, to be sure — are you healthy? are you cute? is there a nuclear war underway? — but time and money are the biggest variables over which you can exercise significant control. For you to be in command of your own life, you must retain that control; you cannot forfeit it to some other individual (e.g., your boss, your spouse) or entity (the government or the bank that holds your mortgage). This is the key to achieving the Leisure Life.

Working Your Life Away

In reality, time and money are not two distinct entities. They are largely interchangeable. The primary reason most of us lack free time is that we spend so much of our lives working. And the foremost reason most of us work is that we need money. (I'm told there are other reasons, such as "job satisfaction." I have found this to be an elusive creature, but at any rate, need for money is the reason most people work the hours they do, at the jobs they do. They would likely choose other work if money were not an issue.) Working comes down to a simple exchange: we trade some portion of our precious allotment of time, ours from birth, for some amount of money. The rate of exchange varies with the job, of course — we all prefer to get as much money as we can for our time — but it is in all cases a simple exchange.

You may never have considered just how big a fraction of your time goes toward earning your income. It's scary when you examine it closely. Let's study a typical 8-to-5 office worker's weekday time budget:

sleeping — 8 hours
working (or pretending to work) — 8 hours
traveling to and from work — 1 hour
showering, dressing, fussing at the mirror — 1 hour
cooking, eating, cleaning up three meals — 3 hours

Now, unless you know a way of stretching a day to more than 24 hours (traversing time zones?), this budget leaves only three hours unaccounted for. Yes, some people get by on less sleep than eight hours a night, and others may scarf their food down like ravenous grizzly bears; but still other people work considerable overtime, or have very long commutes, or literally spend hours primping in front of the mirror. This time budget, with its lousy three hours to spare, is rather representative. And this basic budget doesn't account for such things as shopping for groceries, doing laundry, feeding the dog, paying the bills, or helping the kids with their homework. Anything else cuts into those leftover three hours or is saved for the weekend, destroying that free time as well.

Your job, whether you enjoy it or not, is directly consuming an astonishing fraction of your time. And when indirect expenditures are also accounted for — things like tending to your work wardrobe, or simply recuperating from a crazy day (dealing with work's "Halo Effect") — the cut is even greater. It is work that is the villain in your time budget. To generate large quantities of free time, you have to trim work time. No other item in a person's time budget offers such big opportunity for savings. You can't skip sleeping or eating, not without harming your health. You can't significantly reduce travel time. (It's fun to try, but you end up with those tickets and dented fenders.) And I doubt you want to cut showering or dressing time. Work is it.

The Money-for-Time Exchange Rate

The exchange of time for money can operate in reverse. If you're one of those lucky individuals who already has money coming out their ears, due to inheritance, hard work, or a life of crime, you know there are a number of ways you can buy yourself small amounts of time. Moneyed people employ servants to complete the household chores. They buy new cars every couple of years rather than fuss with old, failing ones.

In fact, most of us exchange money for time on some level. We go to the automatic car wash instead of washing the car ourselves in the driveway. We pay the kid down the block to mow the lawn. We eat out. The extent to which we make such exchanges depends on the degree to which we value our time. How much we value our time depends on how effective we are at making money. In other words, we each have our own personal Money-for-Time Exchange Rate. If you are the president and CEO of U.S. Widgets and Gadgets, with a salary of $2 million per year, it makes sense for you to retain your own chauffeured limousine. On the other hand, if you live in a box by the riverbed, it would be silly for you to hire a cook to heat up your canned pork and beans. The executive has a high Money-for-Time Exchange Rate; the hobo a low one. For all of us, though rates of exchange may differ, time is money, and vice versa.

We have now established certain fundamentals. Working less and playing more comes down to gaining control of one's time and one's money. Managing time and managing money, however, are in large part one and the same. You will be able to increase leisure time by freeing time directly or by freeing it indirectly, by saving money. Saving money will ultimately allow you to work less. (Chapters 5 and 6 will say more on this.) You can also improve your life by saving money for money's sake. Money is a problem solver. Also, a little money — but not a lot — will be required for you to enjoy your leisure time.

WORK LESS AND PLAY MORE

3

Murphy's Law

Most of you are familiar with Murphy's Law. It is usually written like this:

> If anything can go wrong, it will.

I am a firm believer in Murphy's Law; it seems to accurately portray the situation on Planet Earth. But I do have one small gripe with the concept; it is not really a *law*, at least not as it's written above. It just seems to be. When you get a flat tire on the way to work, you say, "Old Man Murphy got me." Especially when it happens in the rain. But think of all those days you didn't get a flat tire going to work. Did Murphy's Law fail? (Perhaps I'm using a bad example here. Some people would be delighted to have an excuse to come into work a half-hour late.) Strictly speaking, then, Murphy's Law should be written:

> Things often go wrong.

Of course, this isn't as snappy as the first version, so you don't usually see it this way.

You will sometimes encounter Murphy's Law expressed another way, one that is appropriate to our present discussion of time and money. This version proclaims:

Expenses equal income plus 10 percent.

(You can find anything you want in one of those 365-day Murphy's Law desk calendars.) I don't consider this version to be law, either. Again, it just seems to be.

Murphy on the Loose

Examples of Murphy wreaking his "plus 10 percent" havoc are numerous and visible. The majority of the U.S. population is in debt, regardless of income level. (Hell, the U.S. itself is in debt.) I can think of many Murphy victims I have encountered; I imagine you can too.

In my graduate school days (1978-1980), most of my compatriots and I were obliged to survive on the proceeds of summer jobs (about $3,000 per year) and on meager stipends from teaching assistant or research assistant positions ($300 to $350 per month, plus tuition waiver). To manage, the grad students doubled up in apartments, rode bikes to class, and cooked with hamburger. Only a small portion had outstanding student loans, and the loan amounts were not typically large (approximately Murphy's stated 10 percent).

By and large the grad students were a happy group. Our classrooms and halls were lively, and evenings and weekends were filled with sports, barbecues, drunken parties, and penny-nickel poker games. (In fact, as I think about it, the group was considerably more upbeat than any I've ever encountered in a workplace.)

Years passed, most students completed their degrees, and the group issued forth into the real world. Within three to four years these young geologists were earning annual salaries of $25,000 to $50,000 (versus $6,000 to $7,000 per year in school). With rare exceptions, though, these young people were in debt. Most had purchased homes, several had children, and virtually all had substantially increased their mass of material possessions. I have to admit that I myself was "barely scraping by" on an annual salary of close to $40,000.

What was the problem? Inflation? True, these were the Carter years. But even three to four years of Jimmy can explain only so much disaster. Could it have been cost-of-living differences between our college town (Tucson, Arizona) and our work cities? Doubtful. Most geologists in those days procured jobs in Denver, Dallas, or Houston, not particularly expensive places to live. (Texas, in fact, had no state income tax.)

Murphy knows the answer. Murphy knows that it's very easy to spend money if you're not careful. Reckless spending can consume a lot of cash, fast. And, sadly, a human being's degree of recklessness seems to rise in proportion to his or her income. The ultimate example of such squandering is the pro athlete who manages to blow an income of six or seven figures per year. Such stories have actually appeared in the newspaper. "Ex-Heavyweight Champ Now on Welfare" and "Star Running Back's House Seized by IRS" are typical. (Does anyone really need to own and occupy four houses?)

In short, money burns holes in our pockets. When I was a youngster of four, my best friend's parents had to dole out his 18-cents-per-week allowance day by day: two cents on weekdays, three cents on Saturdays, and five cents on Sundays. He always marched straight to the candy store with any money he had! But many of us never grow up. Each spring this litany is spoken throughout the land: "Honey, what should we spend our tax refund on this year?"

Unless you have an income barely above the poverty level, you are in a position to save money if you so desire. It is possible to live, and live decently, on a fairly small amount of cash. Most of the things people spend their money on fall under the category of "discretionary purchases." Very little really belongs under the heading "absolute necessities." There is plenty of room for savings. It is important to recognize this. It is important because in so doing, you recognize that the Leisure Life is available. It is only a matter of choosing it.

4

Building a Personal Treasury

The Flow of Money

In a person's life, money flows in and money flows out. The flow out is unavoidable — certain expenses and purchases are essential to life — so a person had better have some dollars flowing in. The days of subsisting off the land and ignoring the rest of the world are gone (unless perhaps you'd like to move to the Amazon jungle, or north of the Arctic Circle).

For many people, the flow of money in is exactly balanced by the flow out (or, worse, the flow out exceeds the flow in, as Murphy describes). Dollars enter these people's wallets or purses and exit them again in a wink. In many cases, these men and women wish desperately that they had more money coming in. They see this as the ticket to an easier life — making so much money they can spend freely and still have piles left over.

It is therefore easy to understand why so many books of the *How to Make a Million Dollars* type are sold. Earning megabucks is great in theory, but as many of you are probably well aware, the advice found in such books can be difficult to follow. One needs to be a sort of all-powerful superbeing to carry it out. And it's very easy to work yourself into an exhausted, stressed-out state in the attempt.

The real answer to getting cash inflow to exceed outflow — and this solution is available to almost everyone — is to cut the outflow (i.e., to cut expenses). It is considerably more sensible to sacrifice a few of the goods and services you spend your money on than it is to sacrifice your time, effort, and even health chasing the big bucks.

Damming the Flow

There is an analogy I'm fond of using when discussing an individual's finances. I like to consider the flow of money in a person's life comparable to the flow of water in a river. The analogy works best if you think of a river in a semiarid region. Water flows into and out of a region much as money flows into and out of a person's life. Water is precious, even life-giving, and let's face it, so is money. When a river is running full, life is good. When it diminishes to a trickle, life is difficult. Ditto for money.

What does a wise farmer or rancher do with an inconsistent river? Rather than suffer its natural ebbs and flows, he constructs a dam across it. During rainy times he uses only the water he truly needs and lets his reservoir fill. Consequently, he has the water he requires when a drought arrives.

Notice that the wise watershed manager does not try to solve his water problems by attempting to increase the flow in the river. It's true that it is possible to "seed" clouds and induce rain, but such techniques are difficult and expensive, and also are not entirely reliable. As a rule, it is wiser to manage the resources you have than it is to be wasteful and expect to discover more.

The message of the river-reservoir analogy is clear: you must dam the flow of money in your own life. You must set aside some money when it is plentiful, because there will be times when it is scarce. You must build up your own money reservoir, your "Personal Treasury."

Income, like rainfall, tends to arrive sporadically. Don't be deceived if you've had the good fortune to have your paycheck come regularly for many years. The rug can be pulled out from under you in an instant. Mergers, cyclical downturns in your industry, changes in tax rules or other matters of law, changes in people's habits or hobbies, the appearance of competing businesses or products — all these developments can eliminate your job security virtually over-night. (I speak from experience here.) But, too, money can arrive in surprise packages: raises or bonuses at work, larger-than-expected tax refunds, lottery winnings or other prizes, inheritances, buried treasure encountered while weeding, etc. (I wish I spoke from experience here.) You need to realize that these windfalls represent unusual, fortunate occurrences and that you should save as large a portion of the proceeds as you can.

A water reservoir filled to capacity brings the farmer a priceless peace of mind. With a brimming reservoir, a type of independence is created. The farmer no longer needs to be concerned over short dry spells. Similarly, when you fatten up your Personal Treasury you develop a type of independence.

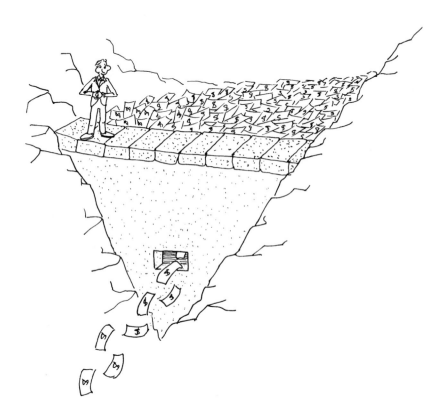

Happiness is a Personal Treasury full to the brim

You no longer need to fear a temporary loss of work. This is no small fear in many of our lives. (A fear which results in us kissing the derrieres of bosses we don't like.)

And something else agreeable falls out of the analogy. It is clear that a full reservoir is a full reservoir; the fashion in which it fills is of no import. A river can feed water into a reservoir at a steady rate or it can fill it all at once in a raging torrent. Likewise for your Personal Treasury: you can build it up in steady fashion or you can toss money into it in lumps. (When I figure out how to fill it all at once, in a "raging torrent," I'll let you know.)

The outcome of this is that once you start employing the Personal Treasury concept in your life, it isn't necessary to continue at a conventional full-time job. As long as you feed funds into the Treasury at an average rate that is equal to or greater than the rate at which you remove funds, you are in good standing. This means that you are free to work part-time, or to work on projects that result in large, lump-sum payments.

The Value of the Personal Treasury

A person doesn't require a tremendous income to build a sizable Personal Treasury. As long as you save consistently — something out of every paycheck — your Personal Treasury can grow quite hefty. Consider an office worker pulling down a salary of $35,000 per year. (Some of you might drool at such a salary, but others may be unimpressed. It seems like a good mid-range figure.) Over a normal 40-year working life — from age 20 or 25 to age 60 or 65 — this person will see $1.4 million pass through their fingers. Check it on your calculator. More than one million U.S. dollars!

If this typical office worker were to save just 10 percent of what she touched, it would add up to $140,000 over her working life. That's a pretty plump little nest egg to have in addition to normal pensions and the like. (I am ignoring the effects of interest accrued and of inflation. These two should roughly cancel.) And if you have a salary higher than $35,000 per year and/or you can do better than saving 10 percent, the figures become considerably more exciting. Damming up that money river, instead of letting it all flow through, can be quite rewarding.

But I'm impatient, and I imagine a lot of other people are too. The idea of having a wad of money at age 65 is nice, but that date is just too far off for me to really get turned on. I worry too much about H-bombs, plagues, and mutants from outer space to let retirement at 65 be my big goal in life. Happily, the Personal Treasury is more than a retirement fund; it has several important uses. And a Personal Treasury of only a few thousand dollars can offer benefits.

The pile of money that is the Personal Treasury serves three major purposes:

1. It can be converted into free time on a grand scale (more on this in the next two chapters).

2. It is a problem solver. Many of those day-to-day aggravations we all must endure —car trouble, appliances on the blink, the sudden need for dental work — are easier to tolerate when they don't represent money problems as well. Thus the Personal Treasury is a stress reducer.

3. It helps you enjoy your leisure time. It buys the little toys we use in our leisure activities — sports equipment, barbecue grills, books, jigsaw puzzles, etc. It pays for movies, concerts, restaurant dinners, golf, and bowling. It pays for food, lodging, and transportation when we travel. (You must

be prudent when spending money under this third category, however. Otherwise it would be possible to spend your entire Personal Treasury out of existence in a flash. More on this subject in later chapters.)

In summary, don't make the mistake of treating your finances like a free-flowing river. Don't simply spend money at the rate that it comes in. If you make this error, the quality of your life will vary with the fluctuations of your income (and the gods of income are a fickle lot!). You must recognize that there is an intermediate step in the statement, "jobs provide for life's expenses." In reality, jobs provide dollars, and dollars cover the expenses. The dollars do cross your fingertips, and you are therefore in a position to manage them, to dictate when and where they will be spent. In good times as many dollars as possible should be piled up in a reservoir, to be held for times when money is harder to come by. Only a fool thinks such tough times will never come.

WORK LESS AND PLAY MORE

5

Achieving
Early Retirement

To my thinking, the greatest benefit of stored-up cash is the fact that cash can be transformed into loads of free time. There are several routes that may be followed in accomplishing this. These paths are described in this and the following chapter.

The Ultimate Goal: Early Retirement

In this country it is commonly accepted that a working person should retire at the advanced age of 65. This popular notion is a vile bit of brainwashing you should endeavor to shake out of your head right now, if you haven't questioned it previously. The idea's popularity probably stems from the fact that the government and many large corporations use 65 years old as their retirement age. Forgive my cynicism, but I suspect they do this not out of any sense of generosity, not because they desire to give a person his or her last good years as a sort of reward, but rather because they consider working folks essentially depleted at that age. (Yes, some people still have a few years left in them, they realize, but not enough people, and not enough years, to be worth going after. Sort of like that last bit of ketchup in a "used up" bottle. Why bother with it? Just open a new one.)

The point is, unless you are fortunate, you don't have a lot of gas left in your tank at the standard retirement age of 65. Mind you, I'm not out to pick on senior citizens here — some people are still very active at 70, 80, or even 90 years old (like that guy I lost to in the horseshoes tournament last August) and I think that's fantastic. But it's not wise for a young person to presume they will be granted numerous vibrant, healthy years after 65. Actuarial tables just don't support this assumption. Sound years after 65 should be thought of as a bonus. I hope you get a few, but I think you should reward yourself before 65, too.

The proper tactic is to take charge of your own retirement. Instead of waiting for government- and industry-sanctioned retirement at age 65, use your Personal Treasury to fund an early retirement. To achieve early retirement, increase your Personal Treasury to a point where you can live on the interest it generates, or on the interest plus a small bit of the principal. (If you fear running out of principal, consider purchasing an annuity at the time you retire. An annuity will pay you for life.) A Personal Treasury of approximately 25 to 35 times your post-retirement annual expenses should be sufficient.

Just how early can early retirement be? It is actually feasible for some individuals to retire on savings from earned income (not from inheritance, etc.) while in their 30s! This is not possible for everyone, of course, but it is certainly an option for many single persons and for childless two-earner couples. Most other people are in a position to save towards a retirement in their 40s or 50s. Achieving early retirement follows primarily from making up your mind to do so, from establishing it as a priority in life.

One Carrot is Captured

Let's switch from theory to motivating example and review the inspiring case of Grant and Darth LeMoine. Grant and Darth are a California couple that achieved a very early retirement. I met Grant during my undergraduate college days at Michigan (Go Blue!); we were roommates for two years.

Grant ultimately acquired a master's degree in electrical engineering, then joined a computer chip manufacturing firm in Silicon Valley. (Silicon Valley lies between San Francisco and San Jose; Silicone Valley is about 400 miles further south.) The work was occasionally rewarding, but as often aggravating. Grant soon concluded that retirement would be a preferred option. He switched jobs twice, enticed by employee stock purchase programs, and built his Personal Treasury. At job number two he met Darth, a human resources representative (talk about "sleeping with the enemy"). Together they realized over $100,000 a year in salary, plus additional cash from sales of company stock.

Their co-workers were making similar sums, but as a rule were spending more. When Grant and Darth bought a two-year-old Honda Accord, their friends Joe and Judy purchased a new BMW. When Grant and Darth moved into a two-bedroom townhouse, Marcel and Macy purchased a 12-room semi-mansion in the foothills. (I was once given a tour of their home. One room was declared off limits to life forms: it contained $30,000 worth of furniture and a furry white carpet. We took turns peeking from the doorway.)

Grant and Darth decided to let one last batch of company stock options mature, then call it a wrap. Grant was 35, Darth 36. By this time, they had garnered nearly $1 million in assorted stocks, bonds, T-bills, and other assets. They moved to Nevada (cheaper rent, no state income tax) and savored the sweetness of life without work. They leased a recreational vehicle (RV), and took to the road. For three years they traversed the highways of the U.S. and Canada. Each of those years equaled a lifetime of vacations for ordinary working folks. As of this writing, they're residing in an apartment again, but venture out on regular vacation forays: in summer 1994 they drove the 2,000-mile Alaska Highway (mountain scenery, abundant wildlife, salmon fishing); in fall 1995 they toured northeast Australia (the Great Barrier Reef, rain forests, the Outback). Next they plan to lease a sailboat and cruise the waters of Hawaii and the South Pacific. Naturally, I have volunteered as crew.

In order to retire at an early age, you must establish early retirement as a top priority, perhaps *the* top priority, in your life. You must follow the steps recommended in this book for cutting your expenses dramatically. You will then be able to place big bucks — thousands of dollars, or even tens of thousands — into your Personal Treasury each year. Once your Treasury has reached a level you feel will cover your expenses for the rest of your life, you too can "drop out" and move to that place you've always dreamed of.

The Decline of Social Security

Unfortunately, there may be one other reason for you to take charge of your retirement financing: other forms of funding may prove undependable. There is some question whether the Social Security system as we now know it will be in operation when you and I reach standard retirement age. Various "prop-up" measures have already been enacted just to keep it viable in the present. Every year, a bigger cut of our paychecks goes to Social Security, and for younger people, the Social Security retirement age has been increased by up to two years. (Congress quietly slipped that one through a while back. Anyone who will turn 62 during or after the year 2000 is affected.)

The trouble with the Social Security system is that it uses inherently unstable "pyramid scheme" methods. (You or I would be arrested for using such techniques ourselves in a business venture.) The money you pay into the system is not stockpiled for your retirement; rather, it is passed on to those currently drawing benefits. There is no "stash" as with your Personal Treasury or a company pension plan — just a giant pile of IOUs to be covered by the next generation of workers. But if that generation isn't as large as the current one (and it's looking like it won't be), there's a problem: too many retirees and too few workers. Something's got to give, and I don't want my prosperity hanging in the balance. Take care of yourself, and you don't have to worry about it.

WORK LESS AND PLAY MORE

6

Semiretirement and Other Time-Off Options

The early retirement option is very appealing, but, you know, I still can't get those H-bombs and mutants entirely off my mind. Retirement even at age 40 or 50 sounds a bit distant to me. What we need are ways to turn money into free time *now*, or in the very near future. Fortunately, options do exist.

A Strong Second: Semiretirement

An attractive alternative to early retirement is semiretirement. If you'd be happy with a leisurely lifestyle in which you still take the occasional odd job, this is for you. The game plan is to fatten your Personal Treasury to a level somewhere between one-eighth and one-half of what would be required to retire early. (It is actually possible for some people to reach this level by their late 20s.) At that point, quit whatever work circumstances you're in, and take a long vacation. After your break, assume just enough work load to roughly maintain the level of cash in your Personal Treasury. You'll be in the delightful position of being able to choose when you'll work and at what. You can pick jobs you enjoy; you can select a variety of employment situations. You won't ever have to worry about burning out. This freedom will be guaranteed by the power of your Personal Treasury. You will never be desperate, and it is desperation that causes us to yield control of our lives to a boss.

I have a pet name for the semiretirement option: I call it the "Travis McGee Lifestyle." Travis McGee is the hero of a series of action/detective novels by the late John D. MacDonald. (The books have a color in the title: *The Deep Blue Good-By*, *The Long Lavender Look*, etc. I recommend them.) Travis is a friendly but tough Florida boat bum who is taking his retirement "in pieces." He spends most of his time lying in the sun or fishing from his houseboat-home, but occasionally takes a case to turn some bucks. In this fashion he maintains his cash supply and rarely worries about the "real" world. I suspect that the popularity of the Travis McGee series stems not only from the quality of its writing, but from the general public's envy of Mr. McGee's lifestyle.

I wouldn't recommend that you try to make your money the way Travis McGee does. But there are numerous ways of making money — good money — part-time. Some industries (the construction industry, for example) employ workers on an individual project basis. Retail outlets add staff for the Christmas rush. Kelly Services and other "temp" agencies work you as often or as seldom as you want. Many companies today prefer to have both permanent and contract or "casual" staff, as a means of dealing with fluctuations in work load.

Almost any professional can set himself up as a part-time consultant. The list of part-time jobs is endless.

If you are willing to travel and/or work in remote places, there are some high paying part-time jobs available (and these assignments can be quite adventurous as well). This is most definitely the case in geology; oil fields and ore deposits are found at the ends of the earth. I've had friends choose assignments in Argentina, Peru, Thailand, Australia, and New Zealand. I was privileged to work a summer in Alaska, exploring for copper, molybdenum, and gold deposits. (This was between years of college.) Having a fat Personal Treasury gives you the opportunity to seek jobs like these.

A lifelong friend of mine (we battled nuns together in grade school) has achieved a semiretired status. Dave Koblenz of Detroit, Michigan, endured for years the rat race of the business world. (Dave has an MBA and a CPA certificate.) He lived simply, renting a room in a house, and invested a large portion of his earnings. Work was stressful, and Detroit winters cruel, but Dave fought on, knowing escape was ultimately achievable.

After nine years, at age 34, Dave had amassed a Personal Treasury of nearly $200,000. He quit work and moved to the virtual heaven-on-earth of Boulder, Colorado (sunshine, scenery, skiing, and a gorgeous college campus). Dave has spent the last five years managing his own investment portfolio (he's made a living wage, and not yet touched the principal). This requires of him only a few hours a day. Otherwise, he enjoys running and biking in the mountain setting, swimming at several area pools, reading, and relaxing with friends. But, most enviably, he has spent the last three summers traveling through Europe, belongings in a pack on his back, train pass in hand. As long as the Dow Jones keeps climbing,

Dave K. finds an acceptable alternative to office life

he'll stick with the status quo. If it flattens or falls, he'll do some teaching or part-time financial work.

The Save-to-Earn Ratio

To give you an idea of the amount of leisure time included in the semiretirement lifestyle, let's toss around a few numbers. Consider a young Ms. Yuppie who is making $30,000 per year after taxes. (Which means she grosses about $200,000 before taxes. I'm kidding, but barely.) If Ms. Yuppie goes hog-wild and buys herself a fancy condo and a sports car, and makes weekly additions to her clothes closet and jewelry chest, she'll spend her $30,000 per year and then some. (I know a young woman like this, named Betty. She owns a 4 x 4 she's never put into four-wheel drive. Last week she purchased a $300 pair of boots and shelled out $120 for a haircut. At present, she has a $10,000 backlog on her credit cards.)

If, on the other hand, Ms. Yuppie demonstrates a little willpower and holds her annual expenditures to $20,000, she will bank $10,000 each year. Her Personal Treasury will grow quickly to a healthy level. After six to nine years ($60,000 to $90,000) she will be in a position to semiretire. At that point, if she continues to save one dollar of every three she earns during work periods (a Save-to-Earn Ratio of one-to-three), she will be able to take off one month for every two she works. Not bad! Right now she's probably getting just two weeks vacation per year. That's one month off for every 23 worked. (Ouch!)

If Ms. Yuppie can reduce her spending to $15,000 per year (and this is quite possible in some parts of the country; my spending was only $10,000 to $12,000 per year during my employ at Shackles Oil), the numbers get even better. Her

Personal Treasury will be at a healthy level, suitable for semiretirement, after only four to six years ($60,000 to $90,000). And after the glorious semiretirement date, she will have to work only one month out of every two, because her Save-to-Earn Ratio during work periods will be one-to-two. Wow!

We thus see that cutting your expenses to the extreme kills two birds with one stone. Obviously, your Personal Treasury grows at a faster rate, but you also find that each dollar in the Treasury is, in effect, worth more, because you know how to live on less.

Admittedly, Ms. Yuppie is in the enviable position of having a good salary and the opportunity to cut expenses dramatically. But almost any person is in the position to choose the semiretirement option at some age well in advance of 65.

By the way, Betty complains she doesn't get to travel enough.

Other Time-Off Options

There are ways to turn even small Personal Treasuries into free time. In a sense, these are just extensions of the semiretirement concept, with greater emphasis on the "semi" and less on the "retired." I will discuss five:

1. **Take time off between jobs.** Job switching is more common today than it was in the 1950s or 1960s. In those earlier years, a worker might spend his entire life at one firm, and a resume showing job switches and time gaps looked awful. Not so in the 1990s. Now companies hire and lay off in alternating years. "I was doing some writing," or "I spent six months in the South Pacific," make for lively interview conversation. Plan on taking a few weeks or months for

yourself next time you're between jobs. Enlarge your Personal Treasury so that next time you find yourself without a job, you aren't bound to immediately start the hunt for a new one.

2. **Request a leave-of-absence from your present job.** If you ask in diplomatic fashion, and considerably in advance of the desired dates, a reasonable employer should grant you a leave-of-absence from your current job (without pay, of course). Even if your purpose is "only" to vacation (a noble pursuit), they should still okay it. Several people have taken leaves from my present workplace, an environmental cleanup company. The "justifications" have included maternity, paternity, overseas vacations, and at-home R&R. Frankly, if your employer won't give you a leave when you ask politely, I strongly question staying with that employer. You only live once (according to western religion); you can't let someone else run your life for you.

3. **Work at a seasonal job.** Some jobs don't continue 12 months a year. If you can land one of these, save your money and vacation during the off-season. Teaching is one such occupation that is widely available. A number of outdoor jobs run only during the warm weather months. Tom, a fellow I met in Alaska, worked there every May through September and took winters off in the "Lower 48." He found jobs in mineral exploration, logging, and commercial fishing.

4. **Employ yourself, and control your schedule.** Self-employed people are in a good position to limit the amount they work, and to arrange their schedules to open stretches of free time. Consultants of all types — engineers, accountants, lawyers — can limit the number of clients and/or jobs they accept. Artists — painters, sculptors, actors — likewise control when they work (unless they fall into the "struggling" artist category, in which case they work constantly and still

starve). If you presently work for a big company, consider quitting and going into business for yourself. The added freedom of schedule might make it worth your while.

5. **Find a government job.** I admit, I was going for a laugh here, but there's a kernel of truth to this. Government workers are awarded every obscure Monday holiday, and typically never work overtime. I honestly do believe government jobs are easier on average than private sector jobs. If you can't beat 'em, join 'em.

7

The Nightmare
Of Credit

The "credit" concept is one of the most obscene and loathsome ever to emanate from the mind of man (up there with integral calculus). The offer of credit by a merchant, or by a bank, is like the "offer" of bait in a trap. To be in debt is to be in a hole — you've lost your freedom. Until those debts are paid, your future is fixed before you. Buying on credit and achieving the Leisure Life mix like kids and Brussels sprouts.

Pause to think about what purchasing on credit means: spending money you don't have. The river-reservoir analogy of Chapter 4 fails to even cover this possibility. Can a farmer irrigate crops with water from next year's rainfall?

Buying on credit is akin to signing a pact with the devil. It's an old and sad tale: Lucifer visits a down-in-the-dumps fellow, and tempts him with riches and worldly pleasures.

The fellow may select anything he wants in *this* world; but, in exchange, his soul will belong to the devil in the *next* world. The foolish man accepts the deal, and requests a Rolls Royce, a suitcase of cash, and a pair of blonde sex slaves. His wish list is filled, and he starts living high. But, ultimately, that awful price will have to be paid, and he'll be sorry. Purchasing on credit is like that — a person lives for the present at the expense of the future. (Incredibly, it is possible to charge the services of blonde "sex slaves" at certain legal brothels in the state of Nevada. Not that I know this by experience, of course.)

A Dollar is a Dollar is a Dollar

The problem with credit is it becomes too easy to spend money. You lose track of a very simple fact, that *a dollar is a dollar is a dollar.* No matter whether the dollars you spend come out of your wallet, out of your checking account, or out of your next month's paycheck via the credit process, a dollar is a dollar is a dollar. (Future dollars may be worth less due to inflation, of course. It is difficult to profit from this, however, because the interest paid on borrowed funds usually exceeds savings achieved by borrowing and repaying later.)

Let me relate a story about a couple who didn't understand the dollar-is-a-dollar reality, the Chumleys of Houston. I met the Chumleys in 1982, when they lived across the courtyard in my apartment complex. I often went golfing with the Mister, who went by the nickname "Chum." Chum and Mrs. Chum were the archetypal consumers. If it was for sale, they bought it. They owned every new gizmo or fad item. And I'd swear they replaced their furniture monthly. (I still have one of their hand-me-down sets.)

One Saturday afternoon, as I was watching the Michigan Wolverines annihilate yet another football opponent, the phone rang. It was Chum, breathless. He was calling to inform me that the local furniture store, Overstuffed Furniture in the Raw, was offering credit of $1,000 to any nonfelon, age 18 or over, who walked through the door. "That's great, Chum," I said. "Thanks for the information. But really, I don't need any new furniture right now, raw or otherwise."

"But Steve," he countered, "you don't understand. We're talking $1,000 credit, no money down, six months to pay!"

Chum didn't understand. That $1,000 he wanted me to spend was real money, just as real as 1,000 one-dollar bills stacked on the table, just as real as a fan of ten crisp $100 bills in my hand, Ben Franklin's face on each. ("A $100 bill saved is a $100 bill earned.") That $1,000 would have to be coughed up eventually, and my Personal Treasury would be $1,000 lighter as a result. A dollar is a dollar is a dollar!

Chum lost his job a few months later (the company he worked for folded), and he and Mrs. Chum quickly found themselves in desperate financial straits. They had to move back to her parents' place until they could regain their financial footing.

The practical lesson of the story is this: always try to think in terms of spending live greenbacks. Even if contemplating writing a check or buying on credit, *think* in terms of handing over hard-earned cash. If you make this a habit, it will help you avoid making foolish purchases.

A person about to order a new car to be paid for "on time," with a several-year loan, can definitely benefit from practicing this approach. Individuals in this situation often squander money by selecting options such as power windows, racing stripes, spoked hubcaps, or the "gold package" of plated logos and trimmings. The true cost of these items doesn't penetrate their brains because the expenditure is spread out over many months; each individual car payment only increases a few dollars. How many car buyers would choose such options if they had to hand over U.S. greenbacks to the dealer on the spot?

Credit Card Crime

Since I don't believe in buying on credit, I'm not terribly fond of credit cards. They do have their legitimate uses, however. Credit cards are handy on trips; they let you carry less cash (though travelers checks will also do). In foreign countries, you'll often get the best rate of exchange if you pay by card. Credit cards are helpful in an emergency, such as a breakdown on the highway. (No, needing a new dress for Friday's happy hour does not constitute an emergency.) Also, many vendors ask that you show a credit card before they'll cash a check.

Always immediately pay any credit balances you generate. Interest rates charged by credit card companies are astonishingly high. They are far above the prime rate, and are therefore far, far above the inflation rate. Quite simply, they are obscene.

Packing credit cards to shopping malls or while out carousing is death. In a few mindless moments, you can spend yourself into the poorhouse. (I wonder if MasterCard would accept "temporary insanity" as a defense?) Unless you can control your use of credit cards, leave them at home. Or better yet, do something really drastic so they'll never trouble you again. (Yes, it's time for another story.)

The Big E Cuts His Losses

In my days at Indentured International, I often had lunch with a fellow geologist known as "The Big E." (Large, athletic people whose first names begin with "E" are invariably given this nickname, out of fear and respect.) E had one especially noteworthy habit: he was constantly borrowing money from people at work. This was not really a problem, at least not a problem of mine, because he always paid the money back. It was mainly a curiosity, because he made as much money as most anybody there. E lived in a modest apartment and drove an economy car, so the explanation for his borrowing didn't lie there.

The Big E's problem was that he was being nickel-and-dimed to death. And it was a credit card that was allowing it to happen. One day, E was in my office, attempting to borrow more money. I didn't mind making the loan, but was curious to understand his constant beggary. I asked him why he was always broke, and it was then he described for me his American Express card follies. (This card is sometimes referred to as the "American Excuse.") E was charging some $300 to $500 per month on this single piece of plastic! These monstrous totals included no hefty $100-plus charges, just a host of $20 and $30 charges: assorted restaurant dinners, rounds of drinks, flowers for his girlfriend. He spent because it was so easy to spend. All he had to do was whip out the card!

I could see there was only one recourse for The Big E. I opened my desk drawer and pulled out a pair of scissors. Handing them across, I suggested, "It's time for an execution." He brought forth the card. With a vengeance, he chopped it into half-inch pieces. These he ceremoniously deposited in the wastebasket. The Big E was saved!

Do you suffer from self-control problems like those of The Big E? Now may be the time to go for the shears. . .

8

Reducing Purchase Costs

Thus far we have established the wisdom of piling up a Personal Treasury, and, in a general way, we've established the fact that almost anyone can save significant amounts of money if they're so inclined. Now it's time to get down to the nitty-gritty. Specifically, where do we make our cuts?

Trimming the Fat

In order to save truly giant piles of cash, we must learn to severely curb our expenses. We need to find a way to do this, however, without removing the fun from our lives. Clearly, it's not worth saving money if our lives become drudgery in the process. We need to find a way to trim the fat, but spare the lean.

Unfortunately, separating fat from lean is not always easy. Every four years, during presidential election campaigns, candidates promise they're going to reduce taxes but maintain services. ("Yes, voters, you can have your cake and eat it too.") Needless to say, this never comes to pass; taxes continue to increase. The problem? That which is fat to the president is lean to the Congress, and vice versa.

The point for us is this: I, Steven Catlin, am in no position to tell *you* specifically what to spend your money on and what not to spend it on. I can't just hand you two lists, "Acceptable Expenditures" and "Unacceptable Expenditures," and expect you to adhere. For me to do so would be naive; it would be a failure to recognize your individuality — that you have your personal preferences. What we're going to do instead is discuss spending motives: we will examine why human beings spend their money. Armed with this knowledge, you will then be able to identify what is fat and what is lean in your own life. Understanding leads to control in most endeavors. Doctors have to understand the human body before they can successfully operate on it; engineers have to understand the properties of materials before they can build a suspension bridge.

This chapter discusses reducing Purchase Costs. "Purchase Costs" are amounts you spend for the initial acquisition of goods or, in some cases, services. Outlays for things like groceries, television sets, automobiles, or tickets to the ball game are included. For the time being, let's exclude any discussion of follow-up costs or, as I like to call them, "Consequence Costs." These are expenditures for such items as TV repairs or automobile tune-ups (many of which are services).

A Wise Purchase, Defined

A wise purchase is one made for sound reasons, and one where you get good value. A sound reason might be "because I am hungry." A foolish reason might be "to impress my neighbors." Getting good value is simply a matter of getting your money's worth. Obviously, buying lunch is a sound purchase as far as the "reason" aspect goes, but if it costs $40, you've been ripped. Getting good value is more than that, though; personal factors come into play as well. Buying an almost-new motorcycle for $1,000 might be a good deal, but if you ride it twice and let it rust in the garage, you've paid $500 per use. Good value, therefore, means good value *to you.*

The Seven Purchase Types

I believe that all purchases can be placed into one (or, in some cases, more than one) of seven purchase categories, according to the purchaser's motive. That is, I believe there are just seven basic reasons people buy goods or services, and these serve to define seven basic Purchase Types. The seven Purchase Types are:

1. **Need Purchases.** These are items you need to maintain life, or to prevent physical misery. Included are food, some type of housing, heating and cooling, medical care, etc. Only *necessary* food, housing, and the like pertain here, however. "Treat" foods, such as fine wines or caviar, belong in another category. (Yes, even Godiva chocolates belong in another category, though these come close to being a true need.)

2. **Investment Purchases.** The assorted vehicles available for storing funds in your Personal Treasury are Investment Purchases. Included are savings and checking accounts

at banks, stocks and bonds (including mutual funds), precious metals, rare coins and stamps, etc. Cash stuffed in a mattress would qualify, though you don't actually "purchase" cash.

3. **Pleasure Purchases.** This is a broad group containing any item purchased to bring pleasure — fun, excitement, happiness, intellectual stimulation — into your life. It includes actual physical toys and games ("toys" in the adult sense, including TVs, stereos, boats, and blow-up Trixie Lixie dolls) as well as purchased activities, such as vacation trips or concerts. Buying a pet dog, cat, or iguana falls here as well (but dog food is a follow-up cost).

4. **Convenience Purchases.** Goods and services bought to make life easier are Convenience Purchases. For the most part, this translates into "goods and services that save you time." (A few Convenience Purchases save you hassle, but if you think about it, most of what we term "hassle" is really time waste.) Included here are appliances — dishwashers, microwave ovens, electric can openers — and other physical items that save us time, as well as a variety of services, such as hiring H&R Block or dropping clothes at the dry cleaner.

5. **Ego Purchases.** This category is really an evil spin-off (the dark side) of the Pleasure Purchases category. Ego Purchases are those made solely for the sake of showing off. Included are all status symbols — oversized houses, $10,000 furs, or outrageously expensive (but nonetheless mechanically unreliable) sports cars. The line between this group and the Pleasure Purchases group is thin, and only you can draw it for your life. It is quite possible that a person might own a sports car as a hobby, as one of the real joys of their life. I have a friend who owns an old Porsche 914. He tinkers with it in the driveway day in and day out, takes it for regular spins in the country, and delights in its speed and handling. In such

a case the sports car would properly be considered a Pleasure Purchase.

6. **Tradition Purchases.** This is a particularly sickening category that is all too prevalent. It includes any purchase made without rational thought, simply to be "normal." Examples are silly household items that merely take up space (many knickknacks, wall hangings, and table centerpieces), unnecessary work items purchased so you'll "fit in" at your job (certain tools or professional journals), and special occasion items that are almost never used ("good" china). Oh, but this category doesn't stop at trivial things; it is my belief that a significant portion of house purchases actually represent Tradition Purchases. Many people who really don't want the fuss of maintaining a house, and don't have families to raise, buy houses because it's "the thing to do."

7. **Guilt Purchases.** This category is similar to Tradition Purchases, but the irrational motive here is guilt. If you buy a house because your parents want you to, and you're afraid to disappoint them, you have made a Guilt Purchase. Many gifts to charities could be classified as Guilt Purchases. Money donated to a cause you're not familiar with, or one you don't care about, because of a feeling of obligation induced by pressure, is a Guilt Purchase. Many Christmas gifts are given because the giver believes they're expected; the giver would feel guilty if they didn't follow through.

Using the Purchase Types Classification

I regard purchases of the first two types discussed — Need Purchases and Investment Purchases — acceptable expenditures in nearly all cases. The only real concern in dealing with these two categories is to get the best possible value for your money. There is really no question that these purchases should be made; you have to eat, you need shelter, you should invest your money.

Purchases in the next two categories — Pleasure Purchases and Convenience Purchases —are "okay, but." Some purchases of these two types are reasonable and desirable, but a certain minimum value for your dollar should be achieved. If you buy absolutely everything that pleases you, as well as every possible convenience gadget or service available, you will soon be broke. You must choose only those Pleasure Purchases and Convenience Purchases that greatly improve your life. Ultimately, you must be the one who decides which purchases these are, though I will offer some guidelines in the coming chapters.

The last three Purchases Types discussed — Ego Purchases, Tradition Purchases, and Guilt Purchases — are the destroyers of your budget, if not your life. Purchases in these categories should be entirely eliminated. The potential for damage by these three is great; many big-ticket items can qualify as Ego, Tradition, or Guilt Purchases. It is all too common for people to find themselves trapped in miserable existences because they (1) can't control their egos, (2) don't think for themselves enough to defy tradition, and/or (3) don't stand up to those who try to pressure them into feeling guilty.

I believe the seven Purchases Types serve to cover all possible initial purchases of goods and services, as long as you're flexible in applying the terms. A friend of mine asked, "Steve, what about someone with a drug habit? Is the latest fix a Need Purchase?" I had to think a moment, but then realized that no, it wasn't. An addict's drug purchases are follow-up costs, a follow-up to earlier, voluntary drug purchases. Those initial drug purchases would be considered Pleasure Purchases, albeit misguided ones. How about charitable donations? In most cases, these would be either Pleasure Purchases or Guilt Purchases — Pleasure Purchases if the giver truly cares about the charity, Guilt Purchases if the giver is caving in to pressure. How about paying income tax? This would be a Need Purchase, at least under present-day circumstances. You *need* to stay out of jail; jail would be physical misery (if all those prison movies are accurate).

As with any classification scheme, there are the usual "fence sitters" and items that belong in two categories at once. Some purchases fall on the boundary between Tradition Purchases and Guilt Purchases. This is not surprising; a Guilt Purchase is typically the result of giving in to some individual's pressure; a Tradition Purchase is just a "giving in" to societal pressure.

Items that belong in two categories at once are quite common. A $40 steak and lobster dinner constitutes both a Need Purchase and a Pleasure Purchase. Yes, you need to eat, but it's quite easy to find a decent meal for six or eight bucks. That extra $30-plus represents an entertainment expense, i.e., a Pleasure Purchase. An item that might be both a Need Purchase and an Ego Purchase at once is a sports car. One can certainly argue that in today's world a person needs a car, but a $100,000 Ferrari is considerably beyond what is called for. If a person opts for the Ferrari as a means of flashing their wealth, it represents a combination Need and Ego Purchase. (This is if the Ferrari is their first car. If it's their second, it represents a pure Ego Purchase.)

There can be danger in mixing purchase motives. Mixing motives can confuse your buy/sell decision making, and cause you to lose money. Perhaps the best example is the purchase of a house as both shelter (a need) and an investment (an investment I'm not very thrilled with, by the way; more on this in Chapter 18). There is simply no guarantee that when personal circumstances require you to move, it will be an opportune time — from the investment standpoint — to sell your house. Conversely, when houses are fetching high prices and the investor in you would like to sell, you may have no wish to move. All in all, you'd probably be better off renting your living quarters, and investing your Personal Treasury money elsewhere.

There is only one person in the position to apply the Purchase Types classification to your life, and that's you. You alone know your personal preferences. You must take the time to analyze your spending. Be honest with yourself. Careful thought will allow you to identify those expenditures you can eliminate without cutting into your happiness. Ultimately, of course, your happiness will be increased, because of the many benefits of a fat Personal Treasury.

9

The Good Guys:
Need and
Investment Purchases

In this chapter we will discuss in detail the two Purchase Types which almost invariably represent judicious purchases: Need Purchases and Investment Purchases. Items in these categories deserve their positions in your budget. There are, however, a few pitfalls to be aware of relative to these two.

Need Purchases

A Need Purchase is one required to maintain life or prevent physical misery. "Maintaining life" means staying out of the grave, literally. "Preventing physical misery" means avoiding the unpleasantness of hunger, thirst, sickness, soreness, excessive heat or excessive cold. A safety item might qualify as a Need Purchase. So might a can of bug repellant bought before a camping trip. Keeping mosquitos at bay certainly prevents physical misery. Paying taxes would be a Need Purchase. Paying your taxes keeps government officials (and ultimately fellow prison inmates) at bay. On the other hand, purchases designed to prevent boredom belong under the heading of Pleasure Purchases.

An easy way to decide if something is legitimately a Need Purchase is to ask the question, "Would a human being in their native state require this item?" I call this test the Caveman Analogy. A caveman's needs were simple: food, water, shelter (a cave), fire and/or animal skins for warmth, and probably companionship (which might also have provided warmth). Your needs are likewise simple — essentially the same things the caveman needed, plus a few items to bring you into the 20th century. You also need food, water, shelter, heat, and companionship. Some of the things that weren't available to the caveman which he could have used include air conditioning (in a hot climate), medical care, education, and probably soap. Today a person might also require a car or other means of transportation, and perhaps a telephone. There are other 20th-century "needs" which are really just (bad?) side effects of civilization. These include summer clothing — required to prevent arrest for indecent exposure — and paying taxes.

I am stressing the narrow definition of Need Purchase because people tend to lie to themselves about what really constitutes a need. People are inclined to tell themselves that every frivolous purchase they desire to make is actually a Need Purchase. Let's discuss a few rules of thumb regarding true Need Purchases.

1. **A true need is never realized while shopping.** If you find yourself experiencing revelations in shopping malls —

"Look at that! Glow-in-the-dark silverware. I need that." — you're kidding yourself. Although glow-in-the-dark silverware might come in handy during that occasional blackout, it's not really a true need. A legitimate need will be realized during your normal, everyday existence. When you do identify a true need, put it on your "to buy" list. When you visit the store, buy only what's on the list.

2. **Buy items on sale only if you were planning to buy them anyway.** This includes buying items for which you have cents-off coupons (a type of sale). Create your shopping list based on what you truly need. *Then* check the ads to see what's on sale. If something on your list is available at a reduced price, super! Otherwise, forget the ads. Mind you, I have nothing against laying in a stockpile of some needed item when it's on sale. What I'm denouncing are those silly "I just can't pass up a deal like that!" purchases. A 50-pound bag of Purina Monkey Chow for $1.29 is no great deal if you don't own a monkey. (Unless perhaps *you* like the stuff.)

An additional comment regarding coupon usage: if you enjoy poring over newspaper and magazine advertising sections, clipping coupons, go for it. But if you consider it a chore, you'd be better off skipping it. It all comes down to your personal Money-for-Time Exchange Rate, as described in Chapter 2. If you consider your time to be worth $10 per hour, it doesn't make much sense to spend an hour clipping coupons to save two or three bucks on a trip to the grocery store.

3. **Avoid buying fancy versions of needed items.** Very expensive "Need Purchases" usually represent combinations of Need Purchases with some other Purchase Type. At the risk of insulting your intelligence, let me offer a few simple statements:

- A chair is to sit in.
- A table is to set things on.
- A bed is to sleep in (for the most part).
- A lamp casts light.
- A car gets you from one place to another.
- Clothes cover your body and keep you warm.

I am repeating these simple truths because so many individuals seem to have lost track of them. Many folks apparently believe that all these items —chairs, tables, lamps, cars — should be showpieces! Such people search all over town to find that "perfect" living room set. No matter that it costs thousands of dollars. This emphasis on artistic merit can get immensely out of hand. In some cases, items are purchased which are not even used for their stated purpose. Exhibit A is the solid oak dining table that sits unused in the dining room while the family eats meals on an "ordinary" table in the kitchen —"ordinary" equating to "reasonably priced and perfectly functional."

The most ridiculous example of this syndrome I've personally encountered is a circumstance I remember from my childhood. The woman living next door to us had a sheet plastic fetish. She kept every item in her living room covered with sheet plastic 24 hours a day (at least in my experience; perhaps I had greasy fingers). I think she imagined she was due for a presidential or royal visit.

The point is, you generally shouldn't pay more than you have to for Need Purchases. If you do pay something extra, recognize that the additional cost should be assigned to some purchase category other than "Need Purchases." If the "extra" falls into the Pleasure Purchase category (you really do enjoy sitting in your $600 La-Z-Boy), it may be money well spent. If the extra falls into either the Ego, Tradition, or Guilt Purchase category, you have wasted money.

Keep in mind there are many ways in which *true* Need Purchase costs can be reduced. You can't avoid energy bills, for example, but you can keep them small by turning out lights and by minimizing use of heaters and air conditioners. (Blankets in the winter and fans in the summer are a help.) You can lower phone bills by making greater use of the mails, and by watching the clock when you do call long distance. I won't list all these consumer tips; most are widely known from newspaper and magazine articles. Just remember, your true needs are few in number, and fulfilling them shouldn't be costly.

Investment Purchases

An investment is a purchase aimed at producing a profit. Many items fall into the Investment Purchase category. There are the standard investments offered by banks and brokerage firms: savings accounts, interest-paying checking accounts, money market mutual funds, stocks, stock market mutual funds. There are the various commodities that can be purchased and sold: silver, gold, platinum, scrap steel, oil, grains, orange juice, pork bellies. There are collector's items: rare coins and stamps, antiques, precious gems, baseball cards, and comic books. (I once collected rubber bands, but there's not a big resale market for those.) There is real estate. I would also include purchases designed to hold their value, without actually turning a profit. (I am ignoring inflation here. You actually need to make some "profit" to maintain your buying power.) Examples would be: noninterest-bearing checking accounts, and jars of money buried in the backyard. In short, any method of storing the funds in your Personal Treasury is an Investment Purchase. If you can make a dollar or two as well, great!

Investment Purchases usually represent wise expenditures of your money. Clearly, though, you want to avoid those that won't hold or increase their value. Therefore, there are a few cautions to be offered concerning Investment Purchases.

1. **Educate yourself before investing.** Unfortunately, there are some very bad investments available. Some of the world's most unscrupulous people have found their way into the investment industry, and they profit by selling low-quality products to the naive. It is essential that you as an investor know something about all items you are considering as investments — enough so you know they are legitimate.

Educate yourself from unbiased sources. The seller of an item *cannot be trusted.* A broker or salesman almost certainly has a conflict of interest. Get your information from knowledgeable friends, from newspaper and magazine articles, and from books. There are many fine books available on investing. Some are general and others cover in detail particular facets of investing. For an excellent overview of available investments, check out the latest in Venita VanCaspel's *Money Dynamics* series. At this writing, her most recent effort is *Money Dynamics for the 1990s* (published by Simon & Schuster). Ms. VanCaspel's books are highly readable; an MBA is not a prerequisite.

Money market and stock market mutual funds are what I favor for my own Personal Treasury dollars. I am able to purchase these funds through a discount brokerage firm (Charles Schwab type). Quality mutual funds can be identified through publications specific to the topic. *Money* magazine, for example, publishes an annual guide to stock and bond mutual funds. I select funds with established track records, and no "front end load" (a commission charged at purchase). I also keep a few one-ounce gold coins in a bank safe deposit box. These gold Maple Leafs (Canadian), Eagles (American), and Krugerrands (South African) can be purchased at most any coin store.

For those of you lacking self-control where money is involved, it is possible to set up a fixed contribution plan through a brokerage house and either your bank or workplace. The earmarked dollars can be channeled into stocks, bonds, or funds of your choice. Also, many workplaces offer the opportunity to participate in 401(k) plans (or other, similar tax-deferred plans) with a selection of investment options. These plans, which resemble Individual Retirement Accounts (IRAs), are usually excellent homes for your Personal Treasury dollars. (We'll talk more about 401(k) plans and IRAs in Chapter 21.)

2. **Choose investments that suit your temperament.** It's difficult to make money with investments if you are emotional about them. Investments range from very conservative (with small, guaranteed rates of return) to very risky (with great potential for profit, but commensurate potential for losses). If risky investments scare the undergarments off you leave them alone. There is a tendency to act panicky with investments that scare you, and panic-selling is rarely well-timed selling.

An investment strategy that suits many people involves dividing eggs among baskets. To execute this, invest part of your Personal Treasury conservatively, part in slightly risky ventures, and part in speculative ventures. Split it in a fashion that gives you peace of mind.

Know yourself as well as know your investments before making Investment Purchases. If you hire an investment advisor to help you, or take advice from a friend, that person should know your temperament and respect it.

    3. **Avoid mixing Investment Purchases with other Purchase Types.** If you mix Purchase Types, it may adversely affect your buy/sell decision making. You may find yourself in the position of having to juggle two motives at once: trying to make money and trying to keep you and/or your family happy. It seems as if making money ought to make people happy, but that may not be the case if it necessitates moving out of your home or selling a favorite collection (coins, stamps, antiques). A person will invest most effectively when he or she is in a position to coolly and logically decide what to buy, and when to buy it and sell it. Investment Purchases should be Investment Purchases only.

A Word on Insurance

    Insurance purchases best belong in the category "Investment Purchases." Most forms of insurance are in reality just bank account insurance. They prevent your Personal Treasury from being damaged or destroyed in the event of a major unexpected expense. Auto insurance, for instance, does not prevent accidents; it only pays the shop to fix your car. Health insurance does not keep you from getting sick; it merely pays the doctor to heal your body. Some forms of insurance are "future" bank account insurance. That is, they protect future income, rather than present savings. Disability insurance provides you with an income if you can't work. Life insurance provides your dependents with an income if you *really* can't work. In all cases, insurance involves spending money to protect money.

    Is insurance a good deal? It's hard to say for you specifically; it depends on how much you pay in premiums and on how much you get back in claims. On average, though, the answer is no. This is because, on average, insurance companies collect more than they pay out. I don't need to cite any fancy statistics to demonstrate this point — just consider: insurance companies are profit-making entities; they *have* to take in more than they pay out or they'll fail. The scary part is, insurance companies have to make a profit *after* paying for all those tall buildings they own, *after* paying for that cute advertising they run, and *after* paying their employees enough to live on. Wow! I'm surprised they pay any claims at all!

The moral of the story is this: *you should self-insure to the degree possible.* You should plan on using your Personal Treasury to square any small-scale financial disasters you might suffer. On average, this will result in an increase in the size of your Personal Treasury. Though you may have to tap your Treasury on occasion to pay a bill, the drain should be more than offset by savings realized on insurance premiums. (Stop and consider: over your long history of owning cars and paying for collision coverage, have you collected more dollars in claims than you've paid in premiums? I doubt it.)

You should still carry conventional, purchased insurance to protect against large-scale financial disasters, disasters that can't be covered easily with funds from your Personal Treasury. Examples of this type of insurance would be: liability insurance on your automobile, fire insurance on your home, high-deductible (catastrophic) health insurance, and perhaps life insurance (if you have dependents). Of course, if your Personal Treasury is still quite small, you may not be in a position to self-insure at all. If this is the case, you may want to carry multiple forms of conventional insurance for the time being.

One additional point concerning life insurance: in my view, there are essentially just two types of life insurance, "term" and "whole life." (Other, supposedly different forms of life insurance have been introduced by insurance companies in recent years, but these new forms closely resemble whole life.) Term insurance is pure insurance; you pay for a certain amount of coverage, for example $100,000, for a set period of time, say, one year. If you croak during that year, your beneficiary receives $100,000. If you don't croak, the money you paid in is gone, period. (You'll never hear an insurance agent use the word "croak," of course. They say things like, "If you should, God forbid, pray not, slip away...") This payment-benefit setup for term insurance shouldn't surprise you; it's the same as for almost any type of insurance. If you don't make a claim against your car insurance during a given year, the money you paid toward that is also history. Nonetheless, insurance companies invented "whole life" insurance.

Whole life insurance is similar to term insurance in that it offers coverage in case the insured dies. But whole life insurance also has a "cash value." If you don't die, your policy can still be turned in for some amount of cash (or you can borrow against it, or whatever). This seems favorable, but there is a catch (Catch 22). For a given amount of coverage, whole life insurance costs considerably more than term insurance. Typically, this extra cost far exceeds the cash value of the policy.

When subjected to close scrutiny, whole life insurance is revealed to be just this: term insurance plus a sort of savings program. Typically, it's a savings program that doesn't pay very high interest. If you feel that you must buy life insurance, I recommend you choose term insurance. And you might as well shop around for the best rates. After all, any company is going to have to pay on a claim, no questions asked!

10

The "Maybe" Guys: Pleasure and Convenience Purchases

Two of the seven Purchase Types can be described as neither complete winners nor complete losers. Purchases that fall in these two categories — Pleasure Purchases and Convenience Purchases — can definitely improve your life. But it is also possible to spend so much money under one or the other of these headings that the net effect on your life is negative. Let's consider each of these categories in detail.

Pleasure Purchases

Most of us spend some portion of our income on products and services designed to bring pleasure into our lives. I call purchases of this type Pleasure Purchases. Life ought to be fun, so Pleasure Purchases are basically positive things. But some moderation should be applied. It is important to get excellent value for your Pleasure Purchase dollars.

The Pleasure Purchase category includes items that range in price from almost nothing to items that cost an absolute fortune. It includes hobby items: from gardening supplies to expensive camera equipment. It includes toys: from Trivial Pursuit to recreational vehicles (RVs). It includes entertainment: from music CDs to trips around the world. It might even include nice clothes and fancy cars, though for some these may be status symbols (Ego Purchases). A person should choose those Pleasure Purchases that bring them the most pleasure *per dollar spent*. The next few paragraphs offer several pointers on how to accomplish this.

1. **Recognize that the best things in life are (almost) free.** There is great truth in this old saying, and very little truth in the notion that enjoyment is proportional to money spent. Simple things are often the best: time with friends or family, a newspaper and a cup of coffee in the morning, a stroll on a deserted beach, a Saturday softball game, a good book, a sunset. Even traveling is inherently inexpensive; only the transportation costs represent an extra. Scenery is free; conversation with fellow passengers is free; museums and parks charge only nominal entrance fees. Before my friend Dave Koblenz departs on one of his Europe jaunts, he clears out his rental room in Boulder, stashes his car and other belongings in a storage locker, and suspends his car insurance. As a result, room and transportation costs in Europe represent no new expense.

Many pleasurable activities can be accomplished at great expense or at slight expense, depending on you. Grant and Darth LeMoine (Chapter 5) spent about $1,300 per month on their RV trip through the U.S. and Canada. Some people spend that amount on a three-day vacation to a resort. Similarly, you and your friends can have a backyard barbecue, or you can head to a five-star restaurant. Personally, I think I'd prefer the barbecue; seems like it would be more fun.

2. **Think of purchases in terms of "Work Time Required" or "Free Time Lost."** This is a nifty way of controlling those discretionary purchases. Think of your Pleasure Purchase spending in terms of either (1) having to work more, or (2) being able to play less (whichever is more terrifying). To do this, determine how much money you clear, not gross, per day of work. Don't count money that's slated for taxes or other unavoidable expenses. (Typically, the amount you clear will be only a fraction of the amount you gross, perhaps one-third or one-fourth.) Henceforth, when considering a Pleasure Purchase, convert the price into Work Time Required. For example, you might say to yourself, "This spectacular water-buffalo trophy head is only $2,000. It would make an impressive centerpiece for the den. Let's see, if I can clear $20 per day, that'd be just 100 days of work . . . roughly from now till February. On second thought, maybe I'll wait and see if someone buys it for me for Christmas."

Alternatively, you can consider your prospective purchases in terms of Free Time Lost. For this, figure the amount you'll need per day to exist after you retire or semi-retire. Henceforth, when considering a Pleasure Purchase, convert the price into retirement days lost. You might find yourself saying, "I can buy the Toyota and retire next year, or I can buy the Rolls Royce and retire in 2012." This kind of thinking keeps your Personal Treasury pleasantly plump!

3. **Think of purchases in terms of Cost-per-Use.** Often people fail to comprehend the miserable value they get for their Pleasure Purchase dollars. One problem is people don't generally calculate Purchase Costs on a per-use basis. Recall

the motorcycle in Chapter 8 that seemed like a steal at $1,000. The motorcycle was used twice, at $500 per use. Such situations are not unusual; I personally know of three people with expensive boats rotting in their backyards or garages.

In some cases, people kid themselves about how much they'll use an item they're considering purchasing. I imagine the folks with the rotting boats pictured themselves fishing or water-skiing nearly every weekend. Such visions rarely come true. Few of us have the play time we wish we had (mainly because we're working to pay for our unused toys). Another example comes to mind: club memberships. I know of people who pay $50 a month for a membership to a racquetball club, and go only twice a month. That's $25 per visit! Heck, you can play tennis (another racket game) for free on a public court.

If possible, calculate the cost of a Pleasure Purchase on a per-use basis. *Then* decide if it's worth your money. Be honest with yourself about how much you really will use a product or service.

4. **Beware of hobbies run amok.** This can be a nightmare! Most of you probably know at least one person who has suffered the hobbyitis "disease." It starts off innocently enough: the victim starts checking their pocket change for old coins, or buys a camera, or signs up for a ceramic class. At this stage, the hobby is a healthy thing, a pleasant diversion from more mundane day-to-day activities. Unfortunately, it doesn't stop there; the hobby grows and grows. Finally, a point is reached where the hobby is consuming nearly all the victim's spare time and money. (Usually, the victim's spouse is consumed too — with rage.)

Sounds like a horror movie, doesn't it? It reminds me of one horror movie in particular, *The Blob,* with Steve

"But I got a great deal..."

McQueen. In this classic film, a blob of outer-space goo crashes to Earth and commences eating people (by enveloping and digesting them). With every meal, the monster grows larger. By the end of the movie, The Blob is huge, and threatens the city. Fortunately for humanity, Steve McQueen kills it with a chemical spray.

If you have a hobby that's out of control, you ought to consider killing it, too, or at least chopping it back. If you have one that's under control, keep it on its leash. Buy only the coins or the photographic equipment that you really have time to enjoy. Resist the urge to become the "complete" hobbyist, according to some standard. You *don't* have to have one of every item in the catalog.

5. **Beware of treating shopping as a hobby, or an "escape."** Great numbers of people (women, especially) shop simply because they enjoy shopping. Needless to say, such a practice is not conducive to saving money. If you must frequent shopping malls (and I realize they are pleasant places to hang out; they're designed to be), take action to limit your spending. Try leaving your credit cards and most of your cash at home.

I've met a few individuals who venture to stores when they feel slightly bored or depressed. For these people shopping is a type of escape, a not-so-cheap thrill. There are certainly escapes that do more harm — alcohol or drugs, to name two — but there are also many that are less harmful. Examples are reading a novel, going to a movie, or going for a drive in the country. If your depression in any way ties back to a lack of money — if, for example, you don't like your job, but haven't got the money to quit — shopping as a "cure" is clearly counterproductive. In essence you'd be spending money because you don't have money — akin to trying to extinguish a fire by dousing it with gasoline!

Convenience Purchases

Convenience Purchases are those products and services you spend money on to save yourself time and effort. This category is similar to the Pleasure Purchase category in that you can spend next to nothing on it, or dole out a king's ransom. If you are extremely wealthy, it's possible to hire people to do nearly everything for you. (If you are that rich, why are you reading this book? Please stop, and send me a check.)

The amount you spend on Convenience Purchases should be based on your personal Money-for-Time Exchange Rate, discussed in Chapter 2. If you make only a few dollars per hour, you should stick to the simplest of Convenience Purchases: mechanical pencils, electronic calculators, electric food mixers, perhaps a visit to an automated car wash. It wouldn't make much sense for you to spend $200 to have someone paint your bedroom, to save yourself five hours.

As with Pleasure Purchases, try to consider Convenience Purchases in terms of Cost-per-Use. A $15 pineapple corer is only worth buying if you eat fresh pineapple regularly. (Maybe you live in Hawaii.) Some time ago, a phone company representative tried to convince me that plain, old-fashioned phone service was not good enough. I "had to have" call waiting, call forwarding, instant call dialing, and bird calling as well. Had I agreed, these additional features would have increased my basic bill (that is, everything but long distance) from eight dollars to $22 per month! A near tripling! And for features I might end up using only one or two times a month. (I'm not much of a bird watcher.) A Convenience Purchase often sounds like a great idea until you convert its purchase price into Cost-per-Use.

There are a few Convenience Purchases that are "unpleasantness savers," rather than time savers. Hiring the neighbor kid to shovel the walk when it's 20 below, or using disposable diapers, fall into this category. Generally, such purchases are reasonable, provided they're not too expensive. Paying your fishing buddy $5 to put your worm on the hook seems a bit much.

11

The Bad Guys:
Ego, Tradition, and
Guilt Purchases

Three Purchase Types are left for detailed discussion: Ego Purchases, Tradition Purchases, and Guilt Purchases. Money spent on items in these categories is money down the toilet. You would do as well to stand on the street corner and hand out cash to passing strangers, as spend on this vile trio. Ego, Tradition, and Guilt Purchases are the forerunners of regret.

Ego Purchases

Ego Purchases are transacted for the benefit of bloated, out-of-control egos. The classic status symbols belong here: mansions, absurdly expensive cars, 15-carat diamond rings.

Other, smaller purchases belong here, too; this isn't just a category where the upper crust squanders money. If a person spends more than is necessary on need items such as housing, furniture, clothing, or a car, they're likely making Ego Purchases. Similarly, if they spend immense sums on supposed Pleasure Purchases — for example, jewelry, furs, or a country club membership — these, too, may represent Ego Purchases.

Pampered egos are far from rare. Anytime I leave home and head into Los Angeles, I am surrounded by dozens of expensive luxury and sports cars. It's difficult to believe each of those luxury cars is driven by a person so wealthy they can easily afford such comfort, or that all those sports cars are driven by people who truly require the speed, power, and handling their vehicles offer. After all, L.A.'s streets are mostly flat and straight, and generally so crowded you can't do more than 20 on them, anyway. No, most of those fancy cars represent Ego Purchases — big ones. The kind that keep people broke and tied to their jobs.

Ego Purchases are indeed common, and for them to be expensive is also the norm. Eliminating Ego Purchases is one of the biggest steps you can take toward achieving the Leisure Life. If you gain nothing from this book besides a thorough distaste for Ego Purchases, I believe you will have gotten your money's worth. Ego Purchases can greatly reduce the quality of your life.

Let me illustrate this last point with a story. It's about a real person who made an Ego Purchase and came to regret it.

On a Monday morning in late 1985, I pulled into the parking lot outside Shackles Oil. As I was climbing out of my car, a fellow oil company slave and friend of mine, Mike, pulled into the space beside me. We conversed as we headed into work, starting with the usual male pleasantries:

MIKIE: Hey, Steve-scum! How come you're late? Wake up in a strange place?

STEVIE: I wish, dogbreath. What'd you do this weekend?

MIKIE: Oh, I had a great time. Three of us went fishing at Surfside. We rented a beach house and caught mega-quantities of fish.

STEVIE: Great! You should have invited me. Say, what'd it cost you guys? [I often ask questions like this.]

MIKIE: Not much: 80 bucks total for two nights — a little over 25 bucks apiece. You know, I wouldn't mind renting that place for about six months some time. I'd fish every day. They let you rent it by the month. Six hundred dollars, I think it was.

STEVIE: Why don't you?

MIKIE: That's a good one. Because I have to work, jerk-bag. I've got bills to pay.

I glanced back at the parking lot. He had bills to pay, all right. Mike had driven to work in a shiny red turbocharged sports car, one that would probably sell for around 25 grand. By comparison, my car, parked next to his, was a $9,000 economy model (with lower insurance costs and better gas mileage as well). Mike was broke, and the full explanation was parked there in the lot. He had made an expensive Ego Purchase, and as a result would be working — not fishing — for a long time.

To top it off, Mike ended up despising his car. It found a second home in the repair shop — no surprise, really, since Mike had failed to consider dependability as a factor while shopping. All that had mattered were looks and power. In the final tally, the results of this one Ego Purchase were: one empty bank account, a series of headaches (Excedrin headache Number 56 — auto breakdown), and a few fish still swimming in the Gulf of Mexico instead of sizzling in a frying pan.

Appearances are important, but only to a point. It is reasonable to want to look nice for your family, your friends, your acquaintances, and your customers. Likewise, it's reasonable to keep an attractive home or car. The problems start when you try to make statements with your purchases, when you set about trying to impress people.

If you don sunglasses, climb into your giant 4 x 4, and rumble down the street thinking, "I'm a stud," that's your ego on the loose. If you put on your designer dress and $5,000 worth of jewelry, and think, "I'm the envy of every other woman," it's the same story. Anytime you try to send messages to the world through expensive possessions, your ego is getting the better of you.

Attempting to impress people with what you own generally doesn't work anyway. Only the shallowest of people judge you by appearance. When I see someone in an expensive car, here's the message I receive: "Look at me. I know how to spend money." Big deal. It isn't hard to spend money; it's easy as falling off a log. *Saving* money is hard. Notice that the message I receive isn't, "Look at me. I *have* money." That's because the vast majority of Ego Purchases are made on credit. Most of those people flashing the big bucks haven't got a dime. Not to imply that having money is in itself impressive anyway. Many people achieve wealth through no real accomplishment of their own; they inherit money, or they marry into it, or they acquire it through some lucky break. In fact, those people who work the hardest for their money are usually the least likely to waste it.

Then there is the great irony of the Ego Purchase: it ultimately comes to bore the owner. The person who makes an Ego Purchase gets their greatest thrill right at the moment of the buy and immediately thereafter, when they first show the purchase off. It's all downhill from there. This phenomenon is known as "Jadedness." A person tends to become "jaded" (dulled) to a fancy item once they've been exposed to it long enough. My fishing friend Mike admitted to me that his turbo sports car ceased to thrill him after a few months. In the long run he could have been driving anything, provided it was dependable transportation. I ultimately became jaded to my Houston townhouse. Once I had lived in it for half a year, it might as well have been a one-bedroom flat.

Unfortunately, the real Ego Purchase addict "solves" their jadedness problem by spending more. This explains why some people buy a new car every year, and why others say they have "nothing to wear" when they have a closet full of clothes. I pity these people; most of them are in debt to their ears.

One last comment on Ego Purchases: the "Urge to Possess" is just a manifestation of a large ego. If you find yourself saying, "I've got to own that," every time you see something appealing, get a hold of yourself. As surely as it isn't necessary to own an exquisite mountain range in order to enjoy it, it's not essential that you own gemstones, paintings, antiques, exotic animals, or lush gardens in order to enjoy them. These delights are available to the public in museums, art galleries, zoos, arboretums, and the like. In fact, public collections of these items tend to be large and nearly complete, better than any collection you could assemble yourself. This logic doesn't just apply to collector's items. If you think the 99XYZ (or whatever) is a great looking car, when one drives by, give it a good stare. After all, it looks the same to you as it does to the owner who had to cough up 30 grand for it.

Tradition Purchases

Tradition Purchases are made by people who don't think for themselves. Such people are not rare; anyone who automatically accepts dogmatic statements, anyone who refuses to question authority, anyone who robotically conforms to societal standards qualifies. You, as an independent individual, should make only those purchases you feel will improve your life. Your decisions should be entirely your own, based upon your own observations and your own logic. When you make purchases because you want to please the "powers that be," because you want to "fit in," because you want to do what is "standard" or "proper," without considering whether or not these purchases really benefit you, you are making Tradition Purchases.

Almost any item can be a Tradition Purchase. If you buy a house because all your friends have bought houses, that's a Tradition Purchase. If you buy a dog "because every family should have one," that's a Tradition Purchase. Likewise, if you buy a Christmas tree, or a set of encyclopedias, or "guest" china, or any item *without deciding for yourself* it's something you want, that's a Tradition Purchase.

Think hard, and I bet you can recall some Tradition Purchases you have made. (I've made some nightmarish ones.) Almost no one thinks for themselves all the time. Unfortunately, there are quite a few people who almost never think for themselves. (They're called "sheep.") Followers are definitely more common than leaders. Conformists are more common than nonconformists. The trouble is, when you let other people make your decisions for you, you end up like other people — working your life away.

Guilt Purchases

A purchase transacted to ease a feeling of guilt is a Guilt Purchase. Guilt has been described as a useless emotion, and I tend to agree. You are savvy enough to know right from wrong, and I'm sure you steer clear of wrong. You know murder is wrong, armed robbery is wrong, and talking with your mouth full is wrong — so you don't indulge in these activities. What is guilt, then? Guilt is what you feel when you do something *someone else* considers wrong. Guilt comes from not living up to *someone else's* expectations (a someone else that may even be dead). How ridiculous! Stop and think whose life we're talking about — yours. Who should be running it? You! Let that other sucker run his own life.

A common example of a Guilt Purchase is a gift given because you perceive it's expected. It might be a gift for the mailman, or for someone that gave you a present last year. Buy gifts for those people you truly care about — good friends and loved ones — and forget the rest. (Gifts you truly want to give are Pleasure Purchases.) Charitable donations can also be Guilt Purchases. Again, give only to those charities you truly care about. Anytime you find your brain saying "no," but your body doing otherwise, you're likely making a Guilt Purchase. Learn to say "no" loudly and clearly, and watch your savings grow.

WORK LESS AND PLAY MORE

12

Avoiding Consequence Costs

We have established thus far that a substantial number of dollars can be saved by controlling Purchase Costs. Often, however, it seems as if money just spends itself: you're a bystander watching as the money flows out of your wallet. The washing machine breaks and you have to summon a repairman (but certainly not the Maytag repairman). It's a cold winter and your heating bills are through the roof. The car needs a tune-up. These monetary outlays seem beyond your control.

But in reality they're not. If you wash your clothes at the laundromat, you don't have to keep a machine in repair. If you live in a modest apartment, heating bills will be small. If you ride the bus, you save on car tune-ups. Very few expenditures are *completely* unavoidable.

What is true is that it's difficult to suddenly stop spending. People commit themselves to continuous spending. The Purchase Cost of an item doesn't represent the total price you will ultimately pay for that item. There are inevitably follow-up costs — unavoidable follow-up costs, which I thus call Consequence Costs. Repairs are Consequence Costs. Upkeep expenses of any kind — routine maintenance, cleaning, fueling, etc. — are Consequence Costs. Any bill you *must* pay now because of a purchase you made in the past is a Consequence Cost (except, of course, Purchase Costs you might still be paying on installment).

Unfortunately, Consequence Costs are not measured in dollars only. Purchased items make demands on your time as well. If you elect to buy a house rather than live in an apartment, you can expect to spend countless hours hanging drapes, painting walls, mowing the lawn, weeding the garden, shoveling the walk, and executing general repairs.

The cumulative Consequence Costs of some purchases are so great the original Purchase Cost seems tiny in comparison. A puppy might have been priced at just $50 initially, but add shots, license fees, years of food and vet bills and you're looking at a bundle. Figure in the incredible amount of time required to feed, bathe, walk, and clean up after your dog and you're really talking a sum. If you like to travel, it gets completely out of hand; you must either bring poochie along (a disaster) or board him (another sizable expense).

I don't dislike dogs. My point is the Total Cost of an item generally greatly exceeds the Purchase Cost. The Total Cost is a triple whammy: it equals the Purchase Cost plus Consequence Costs in both time and money. Always think in terms of Total Cost when considering a purchase. Consequence Costs can't be ignored; if you try, they'll stride right up and slap you in the face.

The Tieback Principle

Most likely you are paying some Consequence Costs today because of purchases made in the past. Is it possible to eliminate any of these expenses? Indeed, some Consequence Costs can and should be expunged. The key consideration is this: to what degree do you value the item that is generating the Consequence Costs? For example, if you love Bowser like a brother, the time and money you spend on him are almost certainly worth it. Bowser represents a Pleasure Purchase of the highest order. On the other hand, if you live alone in a large house, and the house is consuming a major portion of your time and money — to your displeasure — you ought to jettison the place. The house must originally have been an Ego or Tradition Purchase, or perhaps an unwise Investment Purchase.

All Consequence Costs relate to or "tie back" to some initial purchase. The acceptability of a given Consequence Cost depends entirely upon the worthiness of the purchase to which it is linked. (These two sentences comprise the Tieback Principle.) We have already learned how to evaluate the initial purchase: by applying the Purchase Types classification scheme (Chapters 8 through 11). If Consequence Costs tie back to Need or Investment Purchases, they are most likely essential. If they tie back to Pleasure or Convenience Purchases, they *may* be acceptable — if you're receiving good value for your money. If Consequence Costs tie back to Ego, Tradition, or Guilt Purchases, something should be done to eliminate them.

Certain Consequence Costs can't be eliminated, but can be reduced. A fuel bill is a prime example. Your use of electricity and other energy forms depends in large part on the size of your home. You may be surprised at how large a part. Some years ago I was comparing electric bills with my Houston friend, Dan. We were amazed by the figures:

bills for my then one-bedroom apartment:
$12-30/month
bills for my former two-bedroom townhouse:
$30-$100/month
bills for Dan's two-bedroom house:
$60-$200/month

All three residences were completely electric. Dan and I each lived alone, and we both strove to keep our bills low (by turning off lights, etc.). The only significant variable in the comparison was size of residence.

As a rule, large homes spawn large Consequence Costs — in both time and money. Big houses cost more to heat and cool, cost more to insure, and require more cleaning and repair. The same is true of large automobiles; they typically use more gas, and cost more to insure and repair than small cars. Consequence Costs can definitely be a matter of degree.

Always Buy Quality

Once you have grasped the idea of Consequence Costs, it is easy to understand the wisdom of buying quality merchandise. Quality products may have high Purchase Costs, but they tend to have low Consequence Costs. Quality items endure; they rarely need to be repaired or replaced. Their Total Costs are thus the lowest.

You can usually discern quality by look and by feel (though you'll get in trouble looking for quality people this way). Quality products are made with quality materials — pure, strong, solid materials. Quality products display excellent workmanship — moving parts move smoothly, nothing rattles or bends that shouldn't, edges align.

Better yet, ask your friends what they recommend. If you're thinking of buying a stereo, talk to friends who own stereos. They'll tell you whether they're pleased or not. You might also review popular consumer magazines. These magazines conduct customer surveys and carry out their own testing on products. Most libraries carry recent issues.

Keep in mind you tend to get what you pay for. At least, you don't get *more* than what you pay for. Avoid dirt-cheap products; they usually fall apart in a week. It's better to spend $5.00 on an item that lasts than $1.79 on an article destined for the trash.

To summarize, bear in mind that purchases generally cost more than what's stated on the price tag. The initial purchase starts a ball rolling that's difficult to stop. Consequence Costs, measured in both time and money, are automatic. Shoppers should consider Consequence Costs as surely as they consider Purchase Costs. Those who fail to do so will pay for years. A buying spree does more than deplete a bank account; it complicates a person's life.

If you doubt that Consequence Costs have the impact I claim, perform this simple test: on your next Saturday "errand run," consider the origin of each errand. I'll bet virtually all tie back to some earlier purchase. Those purchases sealed your fate on this day.

WORK LESS AND PLAY MORE

13

Skipping the American Dream

Consequence Costs have been defined as the inevitable follow-up costs — in time and money — to purchases. This is in fact only a partial definition. It isn't actually necessary to make a purchase to suffer Consequence Costs. The Total Cost of a "free" kitten is large — almost as much as for the $50 puppy. Prizes have Consequence Costs. So do noncash inheritances. So do birthday and Christmas presents. Consequence Costs should really be defined as the inevitable follow-up costs to purchases *or free acquisitions*.

It's quite amazing, really: it's possible to receive something free of charge and have your life go downhill as a result! Consequence Costs are insidious; they quietly consume extraordinary amounts of time and money. Failure to recognize this aspect of reality has led to many a person losing control of their life.

The other night I was watching a game show on TV. A contestant won a $2,000 grandfather clock, a $300 ceramic elephant, and a $100 giant chocolate bar. The woman was ecstatic. I can't figure why; I wouldn't have been. She obviously wasn't considering the IRS man waiting to talk to her after the show (the government treats prizes as income), nor the fact she would be responsible for shipping the prizes home herself. And then what? She can sit on her elephant, watch her clock tick, and eat chocolate (for months). The words "win" and "free" should not automatically excite you. Always consider the total package.

Dependent Spouses and Kids

And now we arrive at a touchy subject — dependents. I hear howls whenever I offer my theories on dependents. Tough.

Dependent spouses and kids are acquisitions, and they have Consequence Costs. Oh man, do they have Consequence Costs! A dependent spouse requires as much in the way of resources as you do, and kids come darn close. But spouses and kids give a lot, too; they often add great pleasure to your life. The decision on whether to opt for dependents comes down to evaluating this tradeoff.

My gripe with dependent spouses is that most don't have to be dependent. The positive features spouses offer are provided about equally well by independent spouses as by dependent ones. The only contributions stay-at-home spouses uniquely supply is a variety of household services: cooking, cleaning, babysitting, clothes washing, and the like. If these are performed for a large family or for a family with very young children, they represent a significant accomplishment. In other cases, they're no big deal. I was a single adult for many years, and was obliged to maintain a "household" of one — cooking for and cleaning up after myself. I considered it trivial.

The career of homemaker may once have been difficult. But nowadays, with small families, day care, modern appliances, and instant and restaurant food, it's a "career" that doesn't rate. The position is an anachronism. In most cases today, acquiring a dependent spouse is simply a "Tradition Acquisition." In a few cases, it's worse: it's the dependent marriage partner knowingly using the partner that works.

Kids, on the other hand, are by nature dependent. Kids are expensive in time as well as money. Babies are especially demanding. An infant requires almost continuous attention: they need to be fed, they need their diapers changed, they need to visit the doctor, and so on. A baby reduces your freedom tremendously.

The dollar cost of a child is astronomical. The typical child living at home through age 18 requires:

- 18 years of food
- 18 years of clothing
- 18 years of medical care
- 18 years of shelter (their own room?)
- 18 years of odds and ends (toys, bathroom articles)
- 13 or 14 years of schooling

These disbursements total over $100,000. (I've encountered several figures for the approximate cost of a child; this one is average. You might try your own numbers in the list above.) Furthermore, many children stay at home into their 20s or rack up fantastic college expenses.

Every child you raise will lessen your Personal Treasury by over $100,000. This translates into a postponement of your retirement by some five to 10 years. Clearly, having kids is not something to take lightly. Be absolutely positive you want them.

There are a number of wrong reasons for having a child. A few examples are:

- your friends are having kids (Tradition Acquisition)
- your parents want to be grandparents (Guilt Acquisition)
- your priest, preacher, minister, rabbi, or bishop wants more church members (Guilt Acquisition)
- you want your family name perpetuated (Ego Acquisition)
- you think a baby will keep your marriage together (just plain stupid)

There is only one right reason for having a child: you have concluded a child will add sufficient joy to your life to compensate for his or her huge cost in time and money (a reasonable Pleasure Acquisition).

I hope the day arrives when society regards *not* having children as the default circumstance. I grow weary of hearing, "When are you and Daina going to have kids?" A couple should not have to justify or apologize for a decision to not procreate. Let's be blunt: children are probably the single greatest imposition possible in a person's life. Why should the norm be for a young couple to have them?

Obviously, some of you already have kids — and I'm sure you wouldn't give them up for the world. But before you have more, think about the costs. It's possible for a couple with children to plan on retiring soon after the kids leave home, but each child you have postpones that retirement (or semiretirement) a number of years.

For those of you who want kids because they're "cute," consider this: it's possible to enjoy children without having your own. Volunteer to take your friend's kids to the movies. Or take your niece and nephew to the zoo. (The parents will be glad for the break.) Try joining Big Brothers or Big Sisters. Coach Little League. Become a Scoutmaster. (What? You don't have time? Tells you something, doesn't it?)

The Standard Path

Tradition has been fingered as a culprit throughout this book. This is for good reason —mindless adherence to norms is commonplace, and very destructive. The Leisure Life is an option that is available to most people. Yet, because of a tendency to conform, many who could be living it are instead mired in some boring and/or stressful work routine. In most cases, these people (1) went to school, (2) earned their degrees, (3) joined big companies, (4) got married, (5) bought houses, and (6) had kids, all without ever sitting down and asking themselves, "Is this really what I want?"

These steps — school, professional employment, marriage, home ownership, and kids — are the initial steps on what I call "The Standard Path." It is the path to the supposed American Dream. If you follow The Standard Path because it's what you want — you've pondered all your options and have selected carefully — more power to you. But if you head down it unthinkingly, you're in for trouble. In that case, The Standard Path is nothing but a hideous tangle of Tradition Purchases and Tradition Acquisitions, complete with Consequence Costs. Unfortunately, it is easy for a young person to take the initial steps down The Path. It can all happen in a couple of years. Sadly, the Consequence Costs can last a lifetime. Imagine, all that wonderful freedom a person realizes upon reaching adulthood — tossed away in a virtual instant. If you're a young person, look — and think — before you leap.

Is it possible to travel backwards on The Standard Path? Yes, but the going's tough. Reversing course on The Path is like trying to back your car up a one-way street. It's slow and people honk. You can quit a job and you can sell a house. You can even divorce a spouse. Kids? You'll have to wait for them to grow up. When they're 18 you can throw them out. Backing up The Standard Path is difficult, and can cause great anxiety. For some people, it's too much to consider; they seek escape in alcohol or drugs.

Conforming is a cop-out. Conforming is just mental laziness. It's easy to turn your brain off and follow the crowd. Try blazing your own trail; it requires effort, but it's worth it in the long run. Get in touch with your real desires, and act on them. Don't worry about disapproval by others. (Don't fear those horn honks.)

Make certain you consider all your options. Free will doesn't consist of choosing from a few alternatives that have been set before you. Deciding between Yale and Harvard isn't exercising free will. Not until you consider other schools, as well as nonschool options, is free will flying high.

I'll leave this topic with one last observation on the American Dream: of all industrialized nations, the U.S. ranks second from the bottom in amount of vacation plus holidays. Only workaholic Japan is worse. The dream has become a nightmare.

14

The Value of Renting

Renting can be an excellent deal. Yet many people are averse to paying rent. They feel money should be relinquished in exchange for material possessions only — as if the point of life was to accumulate, rather than experience. It's true that money vanishes when you rent, but absent with that cash are all possible Consequence Costs. If your apartment roof leaks, just call the manager. If you get a warped table at the pool hall, choose a different table. You aren't the one who has to tune that U-Haul truck. As a renter, you leave all the cleaning, repairing, feeding, storing, insuring, and replacing to other people while you go on your merry way.

A business's offer to rent is intrinsically honest. The Total Cost is stated up front. Offers to sell, on the other hand, can be deceptive. Only the Purchase Cost is declared. The Consequence Costs hide their ugly little heads during the sale, then reveal themselves later when you have no choice but to pay them.

Almost any item can be rented. A person can rent a place to live — an apartment or a house — and can rent most of what goes in it — furniture, appliances, a TV, a stereo. It's possible to rent scuba gear, or horses, or a tent trailer for camping. You can pay by the month to use a weight room and sauna. A "greens fee" entitles you to a round of golf. You can even rent a date through an escort service. The only things you truly need to buy are consumables — food, medicine, toothpaste, and so on. (I'd hate to be second renter of any of these.)

It is especially wise to rent toys. A person often buys a plaything on a whim, and ends up getting less than their money's worth. Remember Cost-per-Use. If you buy an expensive toy — a boat, an RV, a swimming pool — and use it only a few times, you've wasted your money. It's silly to spend all your time and money on just a few playthings, when there's a world full of experiences of which you can partake.

The Cottage at Petoskey

My Dad once taught me a fine lesson on the value of renting. It was a lesson on Consequence Costs, though he didn't use the term.

The story concerns a cottage in upper Michigan that belonged to my Dad's mother. It stood near Petoskey, about six hours north of my family's then-home near Detroit. It was distant enough that we got up there only once a summer, usually for a week. The "cottage" was really a shack. It was collapsing, and was infested with mice and toads. The kids loved it; my mother didn't.

Renting can be a heck of a bargain

During my senior year in high school, Grandma died and bequeathed the cottage to my father. It wasn't long after that Dad wanted to sell the place. I was appalled: "Dad, how could you? We love that cottage. We go there every year. We fish and catch turtles." Dad explained, "Steve, the property taxes on the cottage are $500 a year. That new pump we had to put in cost $200. Every year, I have to winterize the place. It's just not worth it."

He suggested a compromise: he would sell the cottage, but would set aside a portion of the proceeds for future summer vacations "up north." Everybody was happy (except maybe the guy who bought the place), especially when we realized the types of rental property available in the Petoskey area. Clean, modern cottages could be leased for just $150 per week! These came fully equipped with dishes, pots and pans, kitchen appliances, heaters, even docks — with boats for rent. The only elements missing were the mice and toads. (I was disappointed.) And someone else had to winterize those places. I wondered why my grandmother hadn't sold years earlier.

The Canoe Incident

There are many fine examples highlighting the wastefulness of ownership. One stands out in my memory as especially illustrative.

After I moved to Houston in 1982, I dated a girl called Nasty (not her real name, but definitely her real personality). Early in our association, Nasty purchased a canoe. She reasoned this canoe would help us enjoy the Texas out-of-doors — east Texas being well endowed with bayous and reservoirs. At $250, it seemed like a bargain.

Do-it-yourself isn't worth the fight

The canoe was delivered "in need of some assembly." (Translation: they gave us a hull and 50 loose parts.) While I started reading the directions, Nasty put our little boat together — backwards. (Yes, a canoe does have a bow and stern.) Several days and fights later, we finally had it assembled properly. Upon stepping back to admire our handiwork, we realized we still needed two paddles ($30) and two seat cushion/life preservers ($20). Even then we would only be able to launch in a flood. To transport the canoe to a lake we would need a car-top harness ($15).

The next weekend we prepared to set out and launch our craft on its maiden voyage. It took a full hour to get going. The canoe had to be maneuvered from Nasty's back patio — the only place it could be stored — through her apartment and out the front door. Getting it astride the car proved to be an even bigger pain (literally — I crushed two fingers). On the road, the canoe threatened to slide off the car roof; we had to poke along at 40 miles per hour in the slow lane.

Finally we arrived at the state park that was our destination. Guess what we saw as we pulled up to the lake? A big sign, "CANOE RENTAL: $2 per hour, $10 per day" — by a long row of canoes.

15

Terminating
Time Thievery

So far we have discussed two important methods of increasing leisure time:

1. saving money, and converting this money into free time
2. avoiding purchases and acquisitions which have Consequence Costs measured in time

A third important approach to saving time is eliminating direct Time Stealers. Time Stealers are activities which are utter wastes of your precious time. The Time Stealers that wreak the most havoc in people's lives are Tradition Time Expenditures and Guilt Time Expenditures. You can guess the meanings of these terms: Tradition Time Expenditures result from "sheep" behavior — automatically conducting one's life according to traditional practice. Guilt Time Expenditures follow from excessive concern over the opinions of others — from living your life according to the expectations of others. Both categories should be chopped clean out of your life.

There is a close correspondence in English between time terminology and money terminology. We spend, manage, and budget both time and money. Motives for spending time are largely analogous to motives for spending money. We can thus define Time Expenditure Types in the same manner as we defined Purchase Types (Chapter 8). Two of the "bad guy" Time Expenditure Types were described just above. Other Time Expenditure Types of importance are Need Time Expenditures (sleeping, eating) and Pleasure Time Expenditures. This book is about maximizing the latter.

Tradition Time Expenditures

Some traditions are fun. I enjoy the Christmas season — the lights, the trees, Santa, Santa's female helpers. Traditions participated in for fun are Pleasure Time Expenditures. It's when traditions become boring habit there's a problem. Do you procrastinate buying a Christmas tree until Christmas Eve, then hurry through decorating it? Do you dread the chore of taking it down a week or two later? If so, these activities probably represent Tradition Time Expenditures. Next year, enjoy the Christmas trees in the shopping mall and in your neighbors' windows and skip having your own. Decembers shouldn't leave you exhausted.

One very common Tradition Time Expenditure (and Tradition Purchase as well) is overzealous picture-taking. Not those photos of your kids growing up — those are next to essential. I'm speaking of the "documentation" of trips.

We've all sat through at least one of those tedious sessions: "Here's Hilda and Ethel at the Washington Monument . . . Here's me and Ethel at the Lincoln Memorial . . . Here's me, Hilda, *and* Ethel by the Tidal Basin. A nice young man from Milwaukee took that one for us." Boy, have those film companies got us snowed! Take a few pictures of your family and friends, then enjoy your trip. Leave photographing scenery to the pros. For the price of one roll of film, you can buy an excellent souvenir photo book of almost any tourist spot on the globe.

Guilt Time Expenditures

Guilt Purchases were discussed in detail in Chapter 11. One Guilt Purchase example was the "expected" gift. Buying such a gift obviously squanders precious money. But considerable time can be wasted too. Shopping for an expected gift is a Guilt Time Expenditure. If your secretary is pleasant and capable beyond the call of duty, get her something for "Secretaries Week." If she's lazy and prone to scowling, skip it. After all, you already pay her a salary.

A common Guilt Time Expenditure is "volunteer" work. If you organize a charity or offer your time to an existing one, fantastic. But if you just can't say "no" when someone calls and asks you to "volunteer," that's weak. There are people on this planet who are victims of circumstances beyond their control, and they deserve our help. There are animals and forests that need protection. There are libraries to build. But there are leeches on this planet too — plenty of them. It's up to you to decide which causes are worthwhile. It's also up to you to decide if you have any time to spare.

Other Guilt Time Expenditures include going to parties, weddings, or funerals so you "won't be missed." Some people even attend weekly church services entirely out of guilt, not gaining anything from the service itself.

Terminate time thievery and enjoy more of those things for which you really have a passion.

16

The Value
of Organizing

Organizing saves time and money. Physical possessions as well as certain activities — errands, chores, studying for school — should be systemized. The benefits of organization are evident from the follies of disorganization: a lack of order wastes time and money. Who hasn't spent an exasperating 20 minutes hunting throughout the house for that Phillips-head screwdriver that used to be in the junk drawer? In some cases it's easier to give up and spend several bucks on a new one. (One friend of mine is convinced he has a half dozen hammers scattered around his home.) Have you ever incurred a late charge on a bill that disappeared in the clutter on your desk? Have you visited the grocery store three times in one day because you failed to get it right the first time?

My favorite "disorganization story" stars our canoeing friend, Nasty. Nasty had an incredible proclivity for misplacing her keys. Every departure from the house, she required 10 to 15 minutes to locate her keys. I kid you not — 10 to 15 minutes, every time! (I went two years without catching the beginning of a movie.) She would run around the house eyeballing counters, throwing open drawers, checking purses and pockets, and foaming at the mouth. It was best to keep a low profile when Nasty was foaming, but once or twice I offered the suggestion she pick a single spot for storing her keys — perhaps install a hook next to the door. For these indiscretions I nearly lost vital anatomical parts; naturally, she continued her ways. By now, those 10- to 15-minute periods have added up to weeks of wasted time.

Organizing your Physical Possessions

I'm fortunate in that I have a natural inclination toward maintaining order, most likely due to strict potty training. But you nonneurotics needn't despair — there are some simple rules you can follow to increase the amount of order in your lives. The secret to organizing physical possessions is offered in this old adage:

A place for everything, and everything in its place.

You should categorize your possessions, and choose a place for each category: shoes in the closet, food in the pantry, dishes in the cupboard, and books on the bookshelf. Designate or create places for little things too: tools in a toolbox, spices in a spice rack, pencils in a pencil holder, warranties and instruction booklets in *one* kitchen drawer. Table tops, counter tops, dresser tops, and floors do not constitute "places." Store items in boxes, racks, holders, drawers, envelopes, file folders, file cabinets, and on shelves. If something is trash, "store" it in the trash can. Yesterday's newspapers don't belong on the kitchen table.

Award your most frequently used items the most accessible locations. Everyday dishes belong in easy-to-reach cupboards. (Once-a-year dishes should be returned to the store.) Your childhood butterfly collection can occupy the rear of the closet — or perhaps the trash.

Unless you have some pressing engagement, or are completely exhausted, there is no time like the present to put things in their places. When bills arrive, pay them, and file the stubs. If you buy new socks, unwrap them and stick them in the sock drawer; don't let them sit on the couch for a week. Throw the wrappings and the store bag in the garbage. If you've finished working on your car, return the tools to the toolbox, and the toolbox to the basement (or the garage, or the closet). Organize, and stay organized, and your life will run more smoothly.

Let me provide an example of how organizing possessions can work in your favor. At the beginning of each year, label a new file folder "Taxes — 1997" (or whatever the current year). Through January of the following year drop in tax-related items — receipts, W-2 forms, etc. When tax time comes, you will be able to sit down with your Form 1040 and required attachments (Schedule A, etc.), a calculator, a pen and pencil, and the folder, and complete your taxes in one short sitting — no running all over the house, no racking your brain to recall all possible deductions.

Now that we've reviewed the mechanics of organizing possessions, I'll clue you in to something that makes the whole operation a lot easier. In addition to the old adage, "A place for everything, and everything in its place," remember this new one:

> The fewer items you have to organize,
> the easier it is to organize.

This is a simple but important statement. The truth is, most disorganized people are junk collectors. They are overwhelmed by their possessions. Organizing is a formidable, if not impossible, task for those who own literally tons of junk. No one can organize an 80-drawer mass of possessions into the eight or 10 drawers they actually have. "Dejunking" is vital to organization. We'll discuss Dejunking in detail in the next chapter, after a few words on organizing time.

Organizing your Activities

Lists are valuable aids for organizing activities. Lists serve to keep you from forgetting activities, and to help you order them in an efficient manner. I recommend keeping two "running" (ongoing) lists: (1) a shopping list of needed grocery and household items, and (2) a "things to do" list of upcoming errands and chores. Other types of lists can be useful as well. Schedules are lists of a sort; these can be daily, weekly, or monthly. (Some people write directly on a calendar. I would still consider this a list.)

The running shopping list works as follows: keep a pad of paper in your kitchen. When you notice a staple running low, make a note on the pad. By "staple," I refer to any product you use or eat on a regular basis. This includes not only eggs, flour, and sugar, but cereal, soup, juice, soda, cookies, aspirin, toothpaste, laundry soap, and so on. When you visit the store, bring the list. If you make this a practice, you'll never again dash madly to the corner; you simply won't run out of things. With other approaches, such as creating a shopping list immediately before you leave, you almost always miss something. Two days later it's, "Isn't there any more toilet paper?"

The "things to do" list works similarly. Anytime you become aware of an errand to be run or a chore to be accomplished, place it on the list: "buy new tennies," "fix back gate," "remember Mom's birthday June 5th," etc. When you feel energetic and have the time, examine the list, and pick a couple items from it. Often, two or three entries can be handled at once — say, with a trip to the mall. It's nice to have this list when you find yourself in "one of those moods": you don't have anything planned, but you don't want to just piddle your time away, either. Check your list, and do something productive. When you want to play, you'll be free.

There are many other applications for lists. At work I often find myself heaped with more assignments than any three humans could possibly complete. In these instances, I list all my tasks, and prioritize them (or have the boss prioritize them — a safer approach). Then I start at the top of the list, and accomplish what I can.

The human mind can track only so much. Lists serve to extend the power of the mind; they improve memory and increase ability to efficiently order tasks.

WORK LESS AND PLAY MORE

17

The Law
of Possessions

Material possessions have been taking it on the chin in this book, and rightly so. Possessions complicate life and, in the net, often reduce the quality of life. Possessions typically require:

1. money to buy (Purchase Costs)
2. time and money to maintain (Consequence Costs)
3. time to organize
4. space to store (and space costs money)

Possessions have an inertia. They "tie you down," decreasing your options in life. Possessions clutter your house, apartment, or office, and make it difficult — in some cases, nearly impossible — to move. And moving can often be to your advantage.

Requirement 4 above is a particular burden. Storage space is *very* expensive. People commonly move to a bigger apartment or house simply because they need more room to store their junk. Needless to say, switching to a bigger apartment or house takes bucks; your rent or mortgage payment goes up, utilities go up, upkeep goes up. Over the years, these extra bills can total thousands of dollars (straight out of your Personal Treasury). Some people fail to downsize their living quarters when they should. Couples in their 40s or 50s whose kids have left home are in excellent position to cut their expenses by moving to smaller homes. Many don't, simply because of the phenomenal volume of belongings they've accumulated over the years.

Storage space of all types costs. Boats require boat slips; RVs need lot space. Some people keep a portion of their voluminous possessions in expensive self-storage lockers ("mini-warehouses"); usually the junkiest of junk fills these. Even within the home, the more books you have, the more bookcases you need. The more clothes you have, the more dressers or storage bins you require. Possessions cost, even those that just sit there.

And so the Law of Possessions — a natural law — is realized:

> Each and every possession extracts
> a toll in time and money.

The question to be asked of every possession is, "Do the benefits of this particular object compensate for its costs in time and money?" The answer is "yes" only in the cases of need items, or items that bring you pleasure on a regular basis. All else should go out the door.

Dejunking

My definition of junk is *anything you don't use.* If an item looks new and is supposedly "worth" $1,000, but you don't use it, it qualifies as junk. Junk should be eliminated from your life.

Junk can be sold, given away, or thrown out. Sell junk at a garage sale, through newspaper ads, or to stores that handle "previously owned" items. Selling junk kills two birds with one stone: you eliminate useless possessions and generate cash. Give junk to friends (if they can truly use it) or give it to organizations such as Goodwill or the Salvation Army. If you find it difficult to sell a junk item, or even to give it away, don't fool around — toss it out.

While Dejunking, look at all possessions with a critical eye. Ask yourself, "Is this something that I either (1) need, or (2) enjoy on a regular basis?" If you can't honestly say "yes" on either count, place the item on the "condemned" pile. And here's a tip on being honest with yourself: don't try to predict the future; use the past as your guide. Don't ask yourself, "Will I use this in the next year?" Instead ask, "Have I used this in the past year?"

A friend from Arizona, Quaid Simmerman, employs a novel technique in identifying junk. When he moves, he puts everything in boxes, and hauls the boxes to his new place. In the ensuing months, he unpacks only as he needs to. That is, he unpacks a box only when he requires what's inside. After approximately one year, any box still unopened is condemned in its entirety. (I'm not sure whether this tactic represents a triumph of brilliance or of laziness. Probably a combination of the two.)

Two roadblocks threaten to stymie a thorough Dejunking effort. These are:

1. the "it might come in handy" notion
2. excessive sentimentality

You're right, it *might* come in handy. So what? The savings you achieve those five or so times per year some piece of junk actually comes in handy are simply not enough to offset the costs of storing immense quantities of junk. The completely Dejunked person may indeed on occasion have to buy or borrow some item which the "junk-rich" person already has. These items will cost the Dejunked person 10 or 20 dollars per year. Storing piles of junk can cost hundreds — even thousands — per year.

Ironically, junk savers with the "it might come in handy" philosophy often can't remember just what they've got piled in their basements, garages, and attics. Thus, their junk *never* gets used. In some cases, junk collectors remember what they have, but can't find it when they need it; the desired item is lost in the mess. (Remember my friend with the six hammers.)

Roadblock Number 2, sentimentality, is a normal, healthy human characteristic. It just needs to be kept under control. You can't save *everything* that reminds you of a special time, place, or person. Retain selected sentimental items: a souvenir from your honeymoon, a few photos of loved ones, a letter from an old friend, your child's first drawing (if it wasn't on a wall). It isn't necessary to keep *every* souvenir, *every* photo, *every* letter, and *every* piece of paper your child has touched.

My mother is a great one for unbounded sentimentality. While at home for Christmas a few years ago I was digging through the cupboard seeking lunch. (Digging is the right word; every shopping blunder of the previous 10 years was there.) Among other horrors, I encountered an ancient box mix for lemon tarts. This tart mix was so old that the once-white box had turned a light brown. The price stamped on the top was absurdly low (11 cents, as I recall). My mother would not, however, let me give it the heave-ho. Why not? Seems it reminded her of when she was pregnant with my sister, Elaine. Did Elaine die tragically at an early age? Heavens no, she's alive and well and working in Michigan, at age 32. She produces new sentimental items daily.

Some Dejunking Examples

Your junk is peculiarly yours. I could talk junk for 100 pages and fail to cover your favorite categories. Yet, in many practical respects, junk is junk. A few examples of Dejunking should serve to guide you in reducing your own pile of possessions.

Books. I'm a book lover, yet I don't own many books. I try to read them and pass them along. I recommend keeping only those books you repeatedly use, such as:

- reference books — dictionaries, atlases, textbooks, guidebooks, "how to" books
- inspirational books — philosophy, poetry
- "pretty picture" books

It is possible to reduce "keeper" books so they fit on one or two shelves. Casualties of book Dejunking should include:

- most fiction
- most nonfiction stories (e.g., biographies)
- textbooks that don't relate to your current profession or activities
- "how to" books or guidebooks whose advice you don't use
- other reference books you don't use

Dejunking 101: Fight through the sentimentality roadblock

If your spouse or kids want to read a specific book you've finished, save it for them. But don't save *every* book "just in case." Consider trading books with friends and using the library as alternatives to buying books. Also, some used-book stores will trade books.

Collections. Many people collect as a hobby. Some save coins or stamps, others collect more obscure things — matchbooks, pieces of barbed wire, souvenir pens. Collections have a tendency to get out of hand (Chapter 10). If yours is growing like the national debt, consider a program of increasing quality while decreasing quantity — keep your favorites and sell or trade the rest. If you've lost interest in a collection, dump it. It's become a burden.

Clothes. Most people have too many clothes. If you have a closet that's overflowing, fight your way in there and apply the "have I used this in the past year" test. Toss every "no" on the discard pile. If you encounter a lot of clothes that are out of style, you're probably a fad follower. Avoid buying way-out, fad clothes — they become junk too quickly. Eighty dollars for an outfit worn three times is wretched value for your Pleasure Purchase dollar.

Records, Tapes, and CDs. Be willing to admit your tastes have changed. If you're now into "easy listening" rock, there's no reason to save Led Zeppelin albums from your college days. If you don't play scratched records or squeaky tapes, don't save them. The money you originally paid for something is irrelevant; it's what something is worth to you *now* that counts.

Magazines. If magazines pile up on your coffee table faster than you can read them, cut them off at the source. If you can't manage to read the May issue in May, you're not going to find time to read the May *and* June issues in June. It isn't necessary that you receive magazines pertaining to every hobby and interest of yours, or to your business. If you find yourself quickly skimming magazines out of a sense of obligation, or to prevent falling behind as new magazines arrive, consider canceling subscriptions.

One additional factor to keep in mind when Dejunking: the burdensome nature of possessions isn't only a function of their volume or weight. Fragile items are a particular hassle. Collections of delicate figurines or crystal take more space than a stash of baseball cards. Also, such pieces are difficult to move. And they don't fare well in earthquakes.

The Golden Rule, and Other Pointers

As you attack clutter in your home and office, keep in mind the Golden Rule of Dejunking:

If in doubt, throw it out.

Human nature is definitely to err on the side of *saving* junk. If you find yourself involved in a mental tug-of-war over the fate of some item, that item is almost certainly trash. Toss it, and you'll probably never miss it.

Couples can have a difficult time Dejunking. In the usual case, the two parties must reach agreement for an item to be tossed. Thus, chances are doubled that the "it might come in handy" monster or excessive sentimentality will crop up. Couples must get together and admit that junk is harming their lives. They must recognize the Couples Syndrome and agree to be especially strict during Dejunking sessions.

Some valuable lessons concerning the creation of junk can be learned while Dejunking. As you sort your possessions, take a look at your discard pile. Observe the types of purchases that tend to become junk. Remember these in the future while shopping. For a little motivation, look at your discard pile and think of what those items cost in the first place. Picture a pile of cash on the floor instead of all that junk — a pile of cash you essentially torched.

If this book sells, the Salvation Army will love me.

18

The Ultimate Possession: The House

Home ownership is held in high repute in this country. The dogma is, a home is a fine investment. It serves as a hedge against inflation, and it enjoys favorable tax treatment. Home ownership is also a fundamental component of the standard American Dream. Home ownership enjoys such a fine reputation in this country that a majority of Americans regard it as a major goal in their lives.

Home ownership is not a goal of mine. In fact, owning a home would be a great hindrance to me. It would slow my progress toward achieving my real goals — chief among these, increasing my personal freedom. In my opinion, home ownership has many drawbacks. This chapter is aimed at giving "equal time" to the negative aspects of owning your place of residence (the bankers and real estate agents having had their say).

Your Home, Time Waster and Monetary Sink

A house is a voracious consumer of both time and money. No other common purchase can match it in severity of Consequence Costs. Many weekends that could be spent camping, fishing, or visiting friends are instead spent fussing around the house. Dollarwise, a house is a sink: a virtual pit into which one pours money.

The most obvious dollar cost of a house is the mortgage payment. By itself, this monthly bill typically exceeds the total cost of renting an apartment, taking tax breaks on the house into account. Not much is achieved with this payment, either. It's earmarked almost entirely for interest; only the tiniest crumb goes against principal (until very late in the mortgage term). But that isn't the end of the matter; if you own a home, you must also pay property taxes, insurance premiums (liability, fire), and perhaps a monthly or annual "neighborhood fee" (for community recreation facilities). There are the utility bills — gas, electric, and water — that are higher for a house than for an apartment. (Shared walls keep heating and cooling bills low. And an apartment has no lawn to water.) There are upkeep charges — bug spraying, plumbing repairs — plus dollar costs of painting, landscaping, and the like.

But what frightens me most about owning a home is the potential for giant, unexpected expenses. I've seen this too many times. Our friend Nasty bought a 30-year-old house and almost immediately had to replace the entire plumbing system. Cost: $5,000! She had to scrape this money together only three months after emptying her bank account to make the down payment on the house. My friend Dan had a terrible time with his place in Houston: in the space of one year, the backyard fence rotted through and toppled over

($500); the roof leaked and had to be replaced ($3,000); and the foundation slab cracked. Dan couldn't afford to repair this last problem, so it remains ($10,000 off the appraised value of his house). My friend Roger had to replace the compressor on his central air conditioner. This was about $1,000. You get the idea. The bills for Dan's disasters alone equal two or three years of an apartment dweller's rent.

A house also demands your time. The owner has to mow the lawn, weed the garden, rake the leaves, shovel the snow, and fix the little things that break. A full-size house takes longer to clean than an apartment.

What it boils down to is this: don't be too quick to buy a house; it's not for everyone. Don't buy as a matter of tradition. Don't buy because of ego or guilt. A house should be thought of as a Pleasure Purchase. Needless to say, the usual rule governing Pleasure Purchases applies: don't spend unless you expect to get excellent value for your dollar. Considering the Total Cost of a house, it needs to deliver tremendous pleasure to be worth its price.

Two categories of people might reasonably purchase a home: (1) parents raising kids, and (2) "homebodies" who actually enjoy around-the-house chores. Kids need space, both indoors and out. If you've chosen raising a family as one of your top goals, owning a house is probably part of that package (though it is possible to *rent* a house, or a roomy townhouse). You should realize, though, that the kids-house package is generally chosen in lieu of great personal freedom, at least for 20 years or so. Few people manage to both raise a family and achieve an extremely early retired or semiretired state.

Homebodies puzzle me, but they evidently do exist. I'm puzzled because I can't imagine any person centering their entire existence around their workplace and their house —

Home ownership can be a drag

two buildings located a few miles apart. The world is an immense, fantastic, varied place, filled with things to do and see, and people to meet; I'm surprised anyone can get that excited about a house. But people differ, and apparently some folks prefer puttering in the garden or constructing shelves to just about anything else on earth.

If you're neither family minded nor a homebody, consider renting an apartment as your living quarters. If you can't abide apartments, consider *renting* a house or townhouse. If you absolutely must buy, at least keep it small. Most bills associated with houses increase with the size of the house.

Myths of Home Ownership

Two myths about home ownership persist:

1. The average person needs the amenities of a full-sized home.
2. A house represents a superb investment.

1. **The Need Myth.** Consider your friends and relatives who own homes. Have you ever noticed that despite all the space these people have, they tend to occupy "favorite spots" the majority of the time? The Mister likes to relax in his easy chair in the den; the Missus and kids like to play cards and games at the kitchen table. Truth is, the average home owner spends 99 percent of their time in either the kitchen, the bedroom, the bathroom, or the family room/den. The living room and dining room? They're for "company" (three times a year). The basement, the attic, the extra bedroom? They're for storage (of junk). Most people use only a fraction of the total area of their homes — a fraction roughly the size of your typical two-bedroom apartment! Even backyards often go

unused; if there aren't any children or gardeners in the family, a backyard is just lawn to mow.

If a significant portion of your home just sits, you're wasting time and money. And space that's filled with junk is space that's just sitting. Dejunk and consider downsizing your living quarters. You may be surprised at how easy it is to live in a small place — you really don't sacrifice much.

2. **The Investment Myth.** I've already pointed out the many ways in which a house milks you on a month-to-month basis. But that's only part of the story. A house is expensive to get into and out of. Initiating a home loan is costly. Banks and mortgage companies charge "points" for setting up loans. (One point equals one percent of the loan amount. For example, it might cost three points, or $2,100, to arrange a $70,000 loan.) You also get stuck for a variety of fees — a title search, assorted inspections, and perhaps an appraisal.

Escaping a house is worse. Real estate brokers receive very large commissions for selling homes — typically several percent of the price of the home (thousands of dollars). Often it takes many months to sell a house. This means you either have to stay put (*tiedown extraordinaire*) or, if you move, pay two mortgages at once (incomprehensible squander). Another possibility would be renting the first place out, an enormous pain in the arse.

It's true that some people realize large capital gains on their homes, especially if they luck into a real estate boom. Often these big gains are not what they're cracked up to be, however; upon close inspection, they prove to be small gains or, in some cases, losses.

To illustrate the point, let's take a look at an imaginary Houston couple, Mr. and Mrs. Profit (false Profits), who "made" $10,000 on their home after four years. (This is an upbeat example. I could describe several real Houston couples who lost $10,000, or more, on homes in the 1980s.) In 1979, Mr. and Mrs. Profit purchased a two-bedroom home in a Houston subdivision for $70,000. Interest rates were then on the order of 10 to 11 percent, so the Profits' mortgage payment was a semipalatable $800 per month (including property taxes and insurance). Taking into account income tax breaks, their payment was effectively $575 per month.

In 1983, with the oil business beginning to falter, the Profits decided to skip town (good thinking). Mrs. Profit went ahead to Atlanta to house hunt and start a new job. Mr. Profit stayed behind to sell their home. In just one month, he located a buyer at $80,000, and the deal was closed. On the drive to Atlanta, Mr. Profit was grinning ear to ear. He and his wife had made an easy $10,000.

What's wrong with this story? First, the Profits paid $2,000 in loan origination and other fees to get into their home, and $3,000 to get out. So their $10,000 "gain" is down to $5,000. During their four years in the home, the Profits spent $300 on carpeting, $200 on drapes, $150 on painting, and $100 on a ceiling fan (all free in an apartment). Now we're at $4,250. That month of double rent the Profits paid set them back $650 ($575 payment plus $75 or so in extra utilities). Now it's $3,600. Add in as gain the small amounts they paid against the loan principal, about $400 per year, and their overall gain is $5,200 — just $1,300 per year of living in the home (hardly thrilling considering the work involved).

Still, that is $5,200, free and clear, they wouldn't have had otherwise — or is it? If the Profits had rented an apartment, they could have saved about $200 per month: their rent would have been approximately $425 per month and their utilities would have been substantially less than utilities for the house. That's $9,600 saved over four years, plus any interest earned. That makes over $10,000, free and clear, without any of the hassles of home ownership.

But the Profits were lucky! House prices crashed soon after they left town. Had the Profits waited an extra year or two before deciding to sell their home, its value would have dropped to about $60,000. Even at that low price, it might have taken them many months to find a buyer. The Profits also managed to avoid any surprise expenses — no roof repairs, no replacing the water heater, no dealing with termite infestations.

Yes, you can get burned on a house. House values don't automatically rise. In cities whose economy is dependent upon a single industry, the housing market can shift dramatically up or down. When business is booming, house values skyrocket. When business turns sour, house values fall. Trouble is, those times when you should sell — from the investment standpoint — you don't want to. When you need to sell, the market is terrible.

Here's another nightmare of home buying: the tax advantages of owning a home disappear if you don't maintain your income level (i.e., your tax bracket). If your income dips, the monthly bill for your home effectively rises; you suffer a double hit. If Mr. and Mrs. Profit had lost their jobs for any length of time, their $800 payment would really have been $800, not $575.

Up With Apartments!

For single persons and couples without kids, the primary alternative to buying a home is renting an apartment. Apartments offer several advantages over houses. The apartment complex where I lived in Houston during the mid-1980s included two swimming pools (with girls), a weight room, a tennis court, a sand volleyball court, a basketball hoop, and outdoor barbecue grills. There were four laundry rooms, and basic cable TV was included with the rent. Security guards roamed 24 hours a day, and the complex plumber/handyman (Schneider) could be raised on short notice most any time. For this I paid $225 per month! (Houston's low rents were the silver lining of the oil glut. A few years earlier, rent on a comparable apartment was $300 to $350.)

Some people don't like apartments; they've had bad experiences with them. My guess is that most of these people have never lived in a large, professionally run, modern complex. If you avoid grumpy landlords, seedy neighborhoods, and ancient facilities, you'll do well in an apartment. As for privacy, achieving the Leisure Life will provide plenty of that. The apartment complex will be all yours while everyone else is away at work!

There is one other advantage to renting your living quarters: if you change jobs, you can easily move and keep your commute short. I have friends at work with lengthy commutes from homes they own. They bought while working elsewhere, had to switch jobs, and now spend an hour a day stuck in traffic.

Apartment rents are relatively low because apartment complexes are relatively inexpensive to operate. Owners of apartment complexes benefit from (1) extensive income tax breaks, and (2) economy of scale. An investor who owns an apartment complex can deduct more than what a home owner deducts. Like a home owner, an investor can deduct interest payments and taxes. In addition, an investor can deduct depreciation and upkeep. Also, big investors are in the highest tax bracket, so a given deduction is worth more to them than it is to you or me (much more than it is to me).

For some people, houses represent reasonable Pleasure Purchases. As Investment Purchases, houses leave something to be desired. There are a number of investments other than houses that serve as "inflation hedges." These investments — stocks, money market funds, gold, etc. — don't make great demands on your time, and don't tie you to one place.

19

Simplicity in the Extreme: Minimalism

The previous seven chapters, beginning with *Avoiding Consequence Costs*, have proclaimed the message that complicating life reduces its quality. Possessions drag you down; they consume your time and money. Activities spawned by guilt or tradition steal your time. For certain people, dependents are a mistake; they take more than they give. Many of the "joys" we eagerly embrace early in adult life ultimately cost us dearly. These early errors come back to haunt us. They're manifested as work stress; as nerve-wracking, paycheck-to-paycheck budgeting; as a loss of independence.

If you are young, you can avoid making these life-complicating errors. If you aren't so young, you can avoid making further errors. To a great extent, you can undo mistakes already made. The complexity of your life can be reduced.

Materialism, one of the worst life complicaters, can be rejected at any age. (My 90-year-old neighbor just had a garage sale.)

Keeping life simple, so the individual retains maximum control, is a policy I call "Minimalism." An individual following all of the advice in this book would qualify as a Minimalist.

Minimalists:

- keep possessions to a minimum — just needs and favorite toys
- are either single or have independent, Minimalist spouses
- have no dependent children
- have no burdensome pets
- rent their living quarters
- avoid activities and associations they don't need or enjoy

You may recognize this list as equivalent to the Four Cornerstones described in Chapter 1: (1) minimize possessions, (2) accept no hangers-on, (3) don't own a house, and (4) defend against those who covet your time and money. We have come full circle.

It follows that Minimalists also:

- have fat Personal Treasuries, which help remedy day-to-day problems
- have great freedom of schedule
- enjoy extensive leisure time
- work at jobs of their choosing
- work with people of their choosing

In short, Minimalists live low-stress lives, rich in personal control. Minimalists eschew ruts; they experience the variety of life. In addition, Minimalists are in prime position to achieve early retirement or semiretirement.

Full-fledged Minimalism is not for everyone; it's too extreme. The closer you can approach the Minimalist endpoint, however (on a continuous scale from Minimalist to ultramaterialist, Standard Path follower), the greater your level of freedom.

The Van Man

My Houston friend Dan related a story of a remarkable Minimalist he encountered some years ago in San Diego.

Dan attended college at the University of California–San Diego in the late 1970s. During this period, Dan met a fellow student who actually lived in an ancient van parked near campus. The van was parked legally, and remained in the chosen space for entire semesters. The "Van Man" stored his books and a few other belongings in the van, and used it for sleeping. (San Diego's weather is ideal, with little or no need for heating or cooling.) For meals, the Van Man either ate sandwiches or went to restaurants. He showered and used the rest room in the nearest dorm, and studied in the library. Because the Van Man was on partial scholarship, his tuition was paid; at the end of his school years he departed debt free.

The Van Man was a happy person. He was invariably in good spirits, had many friends, and did well in school. Though I personally would not care to live full-time in a van, I would sooner trade lifestyles with the Van Man than with most harried corporate executives.

The things you *need* in life are few and simple. It's those thing you *want* that tie you down. If what you really want is freedom, try simplifying your lifestyle.

The Darwinian Analogy

Charles Darwin taught us about survival of the fittest among plant and animal species. A plant or animal is "fit" if it is suited to its environment — that is, if it's capable of operating successfully in that environment. The environment of a plant or animal includes all aspects of its surroundings: the climate, the landforms (or undersea-forms), other plants and animals in proximity. Over the millennia, the most successful plant and animal species are those that can flourish despite changes in the environment: the rise of mountains, the coming and going of ice ages, the emergence of new predators. Successful plant and animal species are termed "adaptable." Species that require the maintenance of an exact set of environmental circumstances are fragile; they tend to die out.

The analogy to human existence is clear: if you depend on the maintenance of an exact set of circumstances in your personal environment, you are fragile, vulnerable. You are asking for trouble (and those who ask usually receive). Don't count on retaining your job; don't depend on the economy staying robust; don't expect your car or house to function without needing repairs; don't assume you'll never want to move. In short, don't get out on a limb; limbs break. Remain adaptable.

For 20th-century humans, being adaptable means many things. It means remaining educated and aware; it means being psychologically stable; it means being self-confident.

But in the context of time and money management, it means just two things. To be adaptable, a person must:

1. remain financially liquid
2. remain physically mobile

Don't let your money get tied up, or yourself tied down. You won't be able to adapt to changing circumstances.

Minimalists are people who are financially liquid and physically mobile. Minimalists have large Personal Treasuries, and their Treasuries are generally invested in stocks, bonds, precious metals, and the like — i.e., liquid assets. A Minimalist's wealth is not tied up in a house or in other physical possessions. Because Minimalists lack physical possessions and lack dependents, it's easy for them to move; they are most assuredly physically mobile. It is fair to say that Minimalists are among the most adaptable of people.

Changes in circumstances need not always be for the worse, of course. Financial liquidity and physical mobility may still be required, however, to take advantage of a break. Opportunity may knock someday and you'll be presented with a chance to greatly improve your life. You might receive an exciting job offer, or get a chance to go into business for yourself. But seizing the opportunity may require some ready cash or a move. If you're not prepared, you'll almost certainly miss out. Opportunity has the nasty habit of knocking once and moving on.

I've had opportunities slip through my fingers because I wasn't financially liquid and physically mobile. The worst of these missed chances was during my final days at Indentured International. The merger was due to be consummated soon, and it was obvious that heads would roll. I and others were thus searching desperately for new jobs. Three offers came my way — two exciting and one ho-hum. Unfortunately, the exciting positions were out of town (in Dallas and San Francisco); the dull one was local (Houston). Trapped in my then-unsalable townhouse, I had to choose the latter. This was Shackles Oil, a veritable house of torture.

Strive to be as Minimalistic as is possible for you. It will increase your options in life and, as a result, increase your enjoyment of life.

20

Minimalism and the Cost of Living

Cost of living varies dramatically across the U.S. Three dollars and 50 cents will buy you a hearty breakfast in rural Montana; in New York City, $3.50 won't pay for parking during breakfast. A Minimalist is in a position to take advantage of cost-of-living variations. Being physically mobile, a Minimalist can choose where to live, and change locales as often as desired.

Retired Minimalists interested in squeezing the most from their money should move to regions with low costs of living. Obviously, other factors besides cost of living are important in choosing a retirement home — for example, climate, recreation opportunities, or the availability of Popeye's Chicken. Fortunately, many very pleasant locales have average or below-average living costs. If you're interested in escaping big city hustle-bustle, you're in luck — it's the fast-paced, hectic big cities that typically have the highest costs of living.

Semiretired Minimalists may want to work in one place and spend leisure periods in another. Those costly big cities happen to be where most of the best-paying jobs are. A Minimalist is in a position to work where the money flies and relax where the money lasts. In the mid-1970s, a number of people made large sums working on the Alaska pipeline. Many of these workers packed their money out of expensive Alaska, to the "Lower 48." In the Lower 48 states they were able to live well for many years on their savings. Some workers made six-figure sums during their pipeline stints, then went south and bought small ranches in Wyoming or Montana.

A Minimalist's Geography

There are many hidden nooks in the U.S. (and elsewhere) that offer pleasant living at reasonable cost. Personal preference plays a role in determining "pleasant," so I will offer a few general pointers and let you do the further research. Some information can be gleaned from the reference section of your local library, but there's no substitute for traveling and checking the situation yourself.

The U.S. Department of Labor, Bureau of Labor Statistics, monitors the U.S. Consumer Price Index, or CPI. This agency issues monthly reports containing scads of numbers no sane human would want to wade through. Among the numbers are local area CPIs and breakdowns of CPIs by commodity type.

Key items factored into CPI calculations are:

- housing
- health care
- utilities and fuel
- groceries
- transportation
- miscellaneous goods and services (clothing, restaurant food, beer and wine, movies, street drugs)

Of these items, housing and health care vary the most throughout the country. Utilities, groceries, transportation, and miscellany vary to a lesser degree. (Just kidding on the street drugs.)

The statistics show the most expensive areas of the country to be:

- the big cities of the northeast, within the Washington, D.C.-to-Boston megalopolis
- the big cities of California
- Hawaii

Less expensive are the midwest, the Gulf states, and most of the west.

A Minimalist should also be concerned with state income tax rates, which can vary substantially. Because most Minimalists have sizeable Personal Treasuries, with resultant high interest income and capital gains, annual taxes can be painful. If you are retiring, consider one of the no-personal-income-tax states. A gentleman at the IRS has provided me a list of these states. (Talking to the IRS is like talking to a cop. Even if you initiate the conversation, you still think you're in trouble.) The no-tax states, as of 1996, are Alaska, Florida,

Nevada, New Hampshire, South Dakota, Texas, Washington, and Wyoming.

Some retirees have moved overseas to take advantage of low costs of living and/or favorable currency exchange rates. Typically, these people discovered their retirement locales during work or pleasure travel in earlier years.

Other Cost-of-Living Considerations

Cost of living may vary *within* a given urban area. As a general rule, costs decrease from the city center outward — that is, costs in the downtown tend to be greater than costs in the suburbs, and costs in the suburbs tend to be greater than costs at the outskirts of the city. This trend follows from the fact that downtown is "where the action is." Businesses and many residents like to be located close in. Obviously, for people working downtown, living nearby saves commuting time (the old time-money tradeoff).

Cost of living can change with *time* as well. When I first moved to Texas in 1982, the oil industry was thriving and Houston was an expensive place to live. Now Houston's cost of living is average. One effect of an economic downturn is a lowered cost of living. When unemployment in an area goes up, the average wage goes down. When people move out of a city, housing prices drop. Of course, there is another means by which cost of living can change with time: inflation. When the government prints more dollars, it raises everyone's cost of living.

Vacationing Minimalists take note: the cost of *traveling through* places is closely tied to the cost of *living in* places. Vacationing through the mountains of the northeast, for example, is more expensive than vacationing through the

Rocky Mountains. In the northeast, motels cost more, camp-sites cost more, and restaurants cost more. (Also, the north-east has an irritating abundance of toll roads and toll bridges.) Vacationing in cities is generally more expensive than vacationing in the countryside. Within cities, downtown hotels and restaurants are typically priced higher than those at the edge of town.

Once you've worked hard to pile up cash, make sure your money lasts. Spend your leisure periods in places with low costs of living. Surprisingly, many such places are as nice as, or nicer than, places with high costs of living. You might even be able to perform your work in a low-cost environment. If you are a writer, or a sculptor, or operate a mail-order business, you can live almost anywhere. Pick an inexpensive and pleasant part of the country and "get a move on."

WORK LESS AND PLAY MORE

21

Minimalism and Tax Laws

Minimalists lead simple lives; as a result they file simple tax returns. Because Minimalists rent their living quarters, they have no home loan interest or property taxes to deduct. They also avoid other, nonhousing debts, so there is no advantage in their itemizing deductions. It might seem this lack of deductions would be costly come April 15th, but all things considered, it's for the best. "Tax shelters" do cut taxes, but they usually reduce financial liquidity and cash flow as well. People heavily involved in tax shelters are often rich on paper, but light in the wallet.

In most instances, it's best to pay your taxes and wash your hands of the affair. Think of it as "cutting off the limb to save the body," or "choosing the lesser of two evils." The life-complicating steps you have to take to reduce taxes tend to be worse than the taxes themselves.

401(k) Plans and IRAs

The exceptions to the above discussion, in my view, are the investment devices known as 401(k) Plans and Individual Retirement Accounts (IRAs). Many workplaces, including most large corporations, offer 401(k) Plans. Contributions to a 401(k) are withheld from your paycheck. The amounts are subtracted from the pretax gross. The withheld amounts are not included in the "Wages, Tips, and Other Compensation" figure shown on your W-2 statement, so you enjoy a tax savings.

An IRA is similar to a 401(k), but must be arranged through a bank, brokerage firm, or other financial entity (a mutual fund company, for example). You can contribute to an IRA on a fixed schedule, or deposit lumps of cash into it at irregular intervals. At tax time, you are allowed to total your IRA contributions for the year and deduct the amount on your form 1040 under "Adjustments to Income." This lowers your taxable income, resulting in a tax savings. You do not have to itemize deductions (use Schedule A) to claim this adjustment. The IRA deduction is usually not permitted, however, for persons participating in 401(k) or pension plans at work.

The 401(k) or IRA monies can be used to purchase any or several of a wide variety of investments. These include certificates of deposit (CDs), stocks, bonds, money market funds, stock market funds, and others. Discuss the options available with your employer (for a 401(k) Plan) or bank, broker, or mutual fund manager (for an IRA). As much as 15 percent of one's income can be contributed to some 401(k) Plans. (There is also a 401(k) dollar maximum. This maximum is adjusted periodically for inflation. At present it is over $9,000 per year.) At many workplaces, employers match a portion of an employee's 401(k) contributions. This feature should in most cases be maximally exploited by the employee. (How often do you get the chance to stick it to them?) For an IRA, up to $2,000 for an individual or $4,000 for a working couple can be contributed and deducted annually.

The dollar value of a 401(k) or IRA deduction depends on your tax bracket. If you earned $40,000 in 1994, and contributed $2,000 to a 401(k) or IRA, your federal tax savings would have been approximately $600. You would also have saved an amount off any state income tax you were required to pay. An additional positive is that subsequent earnings *within* your 401(k) or IRA do not have to be reported on your income taxes for the given year (that is, earnings within a 401(k) or IRA are tax deferred).

There are two catches: disbursements from 401(k) Plans and IRAs are taxed in the year of disbursement, and most early disbursements (before age 59½) get hit with a 10 percent early withdrawal penalty.

These catches are not as bad as they may seem. Losses due to early withdrawal penalties are easily overcome. A semiretired Minimalist can take advantage of his year-to-year income fluctuations (and associated fluctuations of tax bracket); he can put money into his 401(k) or IRA during high-income years and remove it during low-income (leisure) years. In this fashion, he trades severe taxation during work years for mild or perhaps zero taxation during leisure years. Yes, he will have to pay those 10 percent penalties, but that's all he'll pay.

By way of example, let's consider a young Minimalist, Lucell Leisure. Lucell worked full time in 1994, earning $40,000. He contributed $2,000 to his IRA, saving himself about $600 in 1994 taxes. If Lucell decides to take most of 1998 off, he'll be able to withdraw the $2,000 from his IRA and finish ahead. He'll have to pay the 10 percent penalty ($200), but regular taxes on the $2,000 will be nil, or close to nil. Lucell's low income for 1998 will keep him in either the zero bracket or a very low bracket.

Even if your tax bracket remains constant from year to year, a 401(k) or IRA may still work for you. Tax deferral alone has advantages. If you deposited $2,000 in an IRA in 1994 and wait until the year 2000 to withdraw it, you will have earned interest on that money for six years. You will have earned interest on the full $2,000 — both your portion and Uncle Sam's portion. "Your portion" is that fraction of the $2,000 that would have been yours after 1994 taxes, had you not established the IRA (perhaps $1,400). "Uncle Sam's portion" is the amount of 1994 taxes you would have paid, had you not established the IRA (say, $600). In other words, you get the use of Uncle Sam's money — money you would have paid in 1994 taxes — for six years. Compounded interest on $600 for six years is a nice piece of change — in most cases, more than enough to offset that much-feared 10 percent penalty.

IRAs and 401(k) Plans are tax shelters a Minimalist can take advantage of and not lose Minimalist status. These investment plans do nothing to hinder physical mobility, and only reduce financial liquidity by a slight (tolerable) degree.

The Ever-Changing Tax Code

Tax laws change constantly. Politicians use the tax code to achieve a variety of ends. Some politicians want to help business; others want to help the poor. Some want to encourage savings; others want people to borrow and spend. As a result, tax laws change with each new administration or session of Congress.

It's a good idea to stay abreast of major changes in the tax code. It might be sufficient to simply read articles that reach the front page of the newspaper. A better approach would be to read a brief tax manual every few years. I'm referring here to a newsstand publication of the *How to Pay Less Tax Legally* sort, not a technical government report. (It might well take a few years to read one of those.) There are some good tax reference books available as well. These are a bit thick and involved to read cover to cover, but are useful for researching specific topics. An excellent one produced annually is *J. K. Lasser's Your Income Tax*, published by Macmillan.

22

Achieving the Leisure Life

If you are 18 years old you're in a fortunate position: you can avoid making life-complicating mistakes. But if you are 25 or 35 or 45, you may already have made the mistakes. And, as we all know, an ounce of prevention is worth a pound of cure.

Still, if the opportunity for prevention is past (at least in part), the cure is definitely worth attempting. This chapter offers a 10-step plan for reducing the complexity of your life, and increasing personal freedom. It is a chapter about escaping "traps." (I'll admit, though, the chapter doesn't quite weigh a pound.)

The Plan, Part One: Preventing Further Mistakes

Step 1. Stop accumulating possessions. Never make another Ego, Tradition, or Guilt Purchase. Be very cautious about making Pleasure and Convenience Purchases. Remember that purchases and acquisitions have Consequence Costs. View every potential purchase or acquisition as a tiny (perhaps not so tiny) ball and chain to be fastened to your ankle. Rent if possible, and in instances when you do buy, buy quality.

If you have self-control problems, haul out your credit cards, take the scissors, and cut them up. Or use an ax. Make sure they're dead.

Step 2. If you're buying a home, reconsider. Squelch any notion that a house is a need or an investment. A house is a Pleasure Purchase — a huge one, like a 40-foot sailboat or a bus-sized RV. If you choose to buy a house, be sure it's because you expect to get your time and money's worth back in pleasure. There is simply no other reason to buy.

Step 3. From this moment on, eliminate Time Stealers. Do not participate in any activity on the basis of tradition alone. Don't let anyone "guilt" you into helping their cause. Time is precious; no one has the right to demand yours.

Step 4. If you're about to get married, pause for reflection. Does your prospective spouse have the same attitudes about money and freedom that you have? Or is he or she expecting to be your dependent? Frankly, if someone had their sights set on me as a meal ticket/home buyer/co-parent, I'd run away so fast my shoes would smoke. (Yes, I'm married. No, I wasn't tackled on the run.)

Step 5. Think of kids as Pleasure Acquisitions. Plan on having children (or more children) only if you believe their immense costs in time and money will be repaid to you in enjoyment. You don't "owe" kids to your parents, to your religious leaders, or to the world. The world is crowded enough already.

By taking these steps, you will increase both your free time and your ability to save money. You will no longer live paycheck-to-paycheck. Instead, you will begin building a sizeable Personal Treasury. As a result, no employer will ever own you again. You will have cut those puppet strings denying you freedom.

The Plan, Part Two: Undoing Past Mistakes

Step 6. Begin a program of Dejunking and organizing. In your spare time attack cupboards, closets, the basement, the garage, the attic, the extra bedroom. (Yes: it requires spending time to ultimately free time.) You might want to attack category by category: this weekend your clothes; next weekend your books; then your dishes; tools; sports equipment; records, tapes, and CDs. Make sure to eliminate any vestiges of forgotten hobbies. In particular, consider getting rid of large unused items — furniture, an old pool table, that ceramic elephant, etc. Work toward reducing your possessions on all fronts. I think you'll find that every item unloaded is a weight off your back.

Step 7. Look critically at your vehicle(s). If you have more than one, do you really need the extra(s)? Perhaps you should sell the one(s) you use less. If you have just one, is it a gas-guzzling behemoth? Is it a sports car that's impractical and expensive to insure? In either case, consider trading in for something more sensible.

Step 8. Look to reduce the size of your living quarters, and to switch from owning to renting. Once you have thoroughly Dejunked, you may not need all the space you have. If you've been living in a large apartment, you can move to a smaller one. If you're in your own house, you can sell and switch to rented quarters. Fortunately, the best time to sell a house is when it's by choice. You're able to take time looking for a buyer (no desperation element); you can avoid selling in an economic downturn; and you can avoid suffering any "double payments" (simultaneous payments on new and old places).

Step 9. Request that a dependent spouse "contribute to the cause." I can see only one reason for a spouse not working: he or she is at home taking care of very young kids. If your spouse is sleeping till noon, lounging with donuts and the paper till 2:00, and shopping till 5:00, while you work, you're being taken for a ride. In fact, you qualify as a Grade A chump. Both of you should be working so that the two of you, together, can achieve the Leisure Life. When one member of a couple gives, gives, gives, and the other takes, takes, takes, you're not looking at a partnership, you're looking at a host and parasite.

If you feel your marriage is part of your "trap," it might be best to get out of it. You don't owe a living to a spouse who gives nothing back. And you're not doing your kids a favor if you're keeping an unhappy marriage together. True, a happy, two-parent household is best for raising children. But a happy, one-parent household is superior to any unhappy one.

Step 10. If you consider your kids part of your trap, there's not much you can do, at least not before they're 18. I've never actually met anyone, however, who regarded their kids as an outright burden. Parents, even divorced parents, seem invariably to rave about their children. I will say this: once kids are 18 or 20 (or through with college) you should encourage their departure from the nest. As adults, they ought to learn independence. It doesn't serve anyone when you let kids remain dependent well into their 20s. From your standpoint, their dependency is a drain. From their standpoint (whether they realize it or not), their dependency is a weakness. It might be good to charge 18- to 25-year-olds living at home a room and board fee. This would create a "transition stage" between total dependence and full independence. I can remember some 15- to 17-year-old kids in my high school who had to pay such a fee.

Take as many steps as you can toward Minimalism. As you proceed, your level of freedom will increase. You'll find yourself with more free time, and you'll see your Personal Treasury grow. Ultimately, you'll be able to retire early or semiretire.

WORK LESS AND PLAY MORE

23

There is an Enemy

After reading Chapters 1 through 22, you might be tempted to conclude you are your own worst enemy in the fight to liberate time and save money. Although there is some truth to this — self-discipline is important in the struggle — it is also true there is an outside enemy. Not a single enemy, but a horde. In fact, there is a world full of individuals and organizations that see you primarily as a resource. Your status as a resource, however, is dependent on your working hard and spending money freely. You are of little value to this group if you're living the Leisure Life, watching your pennies.

The "enemy" sees you as a potential source of money and power. They desire you to (1) work for them, for a low wage, so they can profit from your labors, (2) spend money on their products and services, so they can profit directly, and (3) join their organizations, so their power is increased.

These persons and groups attempt to induce you to work and spend. They seek to influence your actions by taking advantage of certain aspects of your basic human nature. They know you have an ego; they know you are comfortable with what is familiar, traditional, "ma and apple pie"; and they know you're prone to guilt. They also know you need the "approval" of others, that you need to belong. They're aware you need to feel useful, that you "need to be needed." In short, these persons and groups know you are human, and fully exploit the fact.

For this reason, I call these individuals and organizations "Manipulators." On Planet Earth, we live in a virtual "Sea of Manipulation." Learn to recognize manipulation and resist it. When someone offers a product or service that will benefit you, and asks a fair price for it, no manipulation is involved. But when someone tries to trick you into buying an item or service you don't need, or asks too high a price for something of use, manipulation is an issue. Be aware that manipulation is commonplace.

There are four categories of Manipulators that stand out as especially villainous. These are:

1. Madison Avenue
2. salesmen ("salespersons")
3. employers
4. the government

For the most part, these individuals and groups achieve their aims through manipulation. Naturally, there are exceptions: some advertisers, salesmen, and employers are honest and straightforward; they offer fair exchanges of money for services or goods. The government I'm not so sure about.

Chapters 24, 25, 26, and 27 will discuss specific tricks used by manipulative advertisers, salesmen, employers, and government, respectively (but not respectfully).

24

The Manipulators I: Madison Avenue

Madison Avenue tremendously affects the people of this country. Advertisers successfully influence individuals to spend their hard-earned pay. In fact, advertisers induce some individuals to spend every penny they earn — or, worse, more pennies than they make, thanks to credit. Madison Avenue influences people in both obvious and subtle ways. Many people who believe they are immune to advertising — people who scoff at TV commercials — in reality aren't immune; they are affected on a deep level.

The Blatant Crimes

Advertisers are experts. They understand human nature and make use of this knowledge. In particular, advertisers are aware of human purchase motives. (Recall the seven Purchase

Types, Chapters 8 through 11.) Madison Avenue offers to fulfill your needs, to supply investments, and to feed your desires for pleasure and convenience. It also plays to your ego, your tendency to be traditional, and your inclination to feel guilt.

It is not abusive, of course, to offer to fulfill someone's needs or offer them investment opportunities (remember The Good Guys: Need and Investment Purchases). What is wrong is claiming that something is a need or an investment when it isn't. We hear such claims daily: "Hurry! Order now! No modern kitchen should be without the Rambo Slicer-Dicer!" or, "This beautiful, hand-painted 'Iguana and Child' figurine is a limited issue, destined to increase many times in value. Invest now."

One rip-off I see advertised occasionally is a set of five U.S. silver dollars for approximately $100. As a youngster, I was an avid coin collector, and I still pay moderate attention to numismatics. I am aware that common, circulated U.S. silver dollars, as of this writing, are worth only eight or 10 dollars apiece. (And you can bet the farm the people running the ad won't be sending rare-date coins.) One "tip-off to the rip-off" in this instance is the fact that the silver dollar ads don't appear in numismatic publications; rather, they appear in general publications (e.g., newspapers) where they will reach naive noncollectors.

Appeals by advertisers to our desires for pleasure or convenience (The "Maybe" Guys: Pleasure and Convenience Purchases) are often straightforward (nonmanipulative). Advertisers that honestly inform us what we'll get for our money are worth our respect. Be wary, though, of Convenience Purchases that may fail to do all they're supposed to do. Those demonstrations you see in commercials are arranged under ideal circumstances. Sure, that little vacuum sweeper sucks up loose crumbs — try it on dog hair or dried mud.

Ads that play to ego, tradition, or guilt (The Bad Guys) disturb me. The other day I was subjected to a radio ad for a local jewelry store. The announcer was describing an "unbelievable" jewelry sale in progress. (The reason prices could be slashed so much is they were outrageous in the first place.) In the background, a woman kept singing, "Look at me. Look at me." Imagine, spending thousands of dollars on some tiny bits of stone and metal that fasten to your body! It's pure ego on the buyer's part, and pure manipulation thereof on the advertiser's.

How about this radio ad, by a home builder: A couple is congratulating themselves on their purchase of a new, giant home in southwest Houston. Are they pleased with the features of the house? Do they like the neighborhood? We aren't told. Here's what we're fed:

WIFE: Oh darling, we finally made it — our own giant home. [Tradition]
HUSBAND: Yes, dear. It's all we've worked for. Our friends will be so envious. [Ego]

No mention is made of the fact that the giant home is affordable because it's been built on farm land two hours from downtown Houston.

Madison Avenue is quite adept at using guilt. They promote holidays so you feel terrible if you don't spend your life savings on presents. But it doesn't stop at Mother's Day and Christmas. Now they're cramming Sweetest Day, Grandparents Day, and Secretaries Week down our throats. Next it will be Dentists Day and Landlords Week.

People get suckered by advertisers that seize upon their anxieties and physical imperfections. If you've got a weakness, there's somebody somewhere who's got the "cure." For just a few bucks, sent irrevocably through the mail, you can grow hair on your bald spot, lose 20 pounds overnight, quit smoking, become a "D" cup, or be eternally saved. Want to make a quick million? Just offer one pill that does all five. Collect your dough, move, and change your name. (On second thought, you better make one pill for the men and another for the women.)

There are countless people with advice on how you should spend your money, and very few who tell you to save it. Understand that this is the way of the world, and be appropriately suspicious.

The Subtle Crimes

The advertising ploys just described are annoying, but they aren't the worst Madison Avenue has to offer. The tricks cited above are fairly easy to discern. If you remain vigilant, you won't fall dupe. What makes Madison Avenue a formidable adversary is its ability to subtly dictate American lifestyle and define "success" in America. Let's consider sports car ads. Individually, the ads say, "buy this particular car." Collectively, however, they make the statement, "You're an incredible person if you drive a sports car. You'll get the girls (or the guys). You'll be universally admired." After a few repetitions, people start to believe this load of bull.

Here is the gist of Madison Avenue's message to its audience:

> Your worth as a human being depends on
> what you own and what you consume.

It's tough to get a word in edgewise with Madison Avenue talking

This is preposterous. Success is achieving happiness; a successful person is one who enjoys life. I believe a person enjoys life when they (1) maximize activities they relish, and (2) minimize activities they dislike.

There was a TV ad campaign approximately five years ago I greatly despised. It was a series of commercials for a certain brand of beer. The ads informed us, "You can have it all," and showed beautiful young adults at work and enthusiastic play. (Somehow this beer provided both the looks and the boundless energy.) Imagine that, you — an everyday, normal guy or gal — can have it all! You can work hard, and you can play hard. You can be a phenomenal success at every single thing you try. And you can fly to the moon with ostrich feathers taped to your arms.

The truth is, you can't have it all. Maybe Bill Gates can have it all. But you and I can't. Life for most people involves choices. You can pick A, B, or C, but not D, "all of the above." I've yet to meet a "success" at the office who had any time left for anything else. Most of my "moderately successful" friends work 40- to 50-hour weeks and are exhausted by Friday. They require the weekend to recover.

Another irksome TV commercial exhibited a tall, handsome executive sauntering down the broad steps of a public building with his "All American" family in tow (one pretty wife, one clean-cut teenage son, one cute young daughter). They're ostensibly on a family outing. The man tells us he owns his own business, he owns his own sailboat, he owns his own this, that, and the other —but, mind you, he leases his luxury car, blah, blah, blah. What bothers me about this commercial is the fantasy image of the "successful man." Most business owners I'm familiar with are workaholics. Yes, they own some expensive items, but they have almost no time for family outings to the museum or for sailing. (Have you ever noticed, on visits to a marina, how few empty slips you see, even on a lovely day?)

The path in life that leads to the standard American Dream — to "success" at work, the big family, the sprawling house in the suburbs, the several new or nearly new cars in the driveway — is an altogether different path from the one that leads to the Leisure Life. You travel one route or the other, not both. Early in adult life you encounter the fork and have to choose. Don't let Madison Avenue tell you otherwise.

WORK LESS AND PLAY MORE

25

The Manipulators II: Salesmen

I'll start this chapter by stating that I've met a number of decent salesmen in my life — honest, aboveboard human beings who treat their customers and potential customers with respect. Encounters with decent salesmen are a relative delight. One almost wants to make a purchase from an honest salesman, just to "reward" them for being sincere.

This chapter is about the other two-thirds of salesmen — the slime. These charlatans will do virtually anything to make a sale. Many slime salesmen have no code of honor whatsoever. These snakes will not only exaggerate and relate half-truths, they will lie outright.

Snakes in the Grass

To understand the variety of foul tactics salesmen may employ, let me relate a few specific incidents.

• In fall 1982, I was townhouse hunting in southwest Houston. (Forgive me; I was young.) One stop in my search was the Riverswill Condominium complex, still under construction. At Riverswill, I encountered one of the foulest human beings ever to inhabit the planet. In his sales pitch, this slug informed me that (1) townhouses in southwest Houston were increasing in value by $1,000 per month, and could be expected to do so for at least two more years; (2) the Riverswill Condominium project was the last condo/townhouse complex that would ever be built within 10 minutes of where we were standing (according to Sluggo, other vacant lots in the region were slated for office buildings, shopping centers, or parks); and (3) a $250 deposit would hold a unit in the complex for me while I completed my shopping. I would be able to get my $250 back within 24 hours at absolutely any time by making one phone call.

Need I even finish this story? I ended up buying a townhouse elsewhere, about four miles from Riverswill. Within two years, (1) townhouses in the area had lost 40 percent of their value; and (2) six or eight large condo/townhouse complexes had been built between my place and the Riverswill development. Also, (3) it had taken several months and approximately 25 phone calls, including to the Better Business Bureau and the Texas Attorney General's office, to get my $250 back. In case you'd like to dismiss this story as an exception, consider this: Riverswill was built and marketed by one of the nation's largest building companies, not by a two-bit, local operation.

- Also in fall 1982, my ex-girlfriend, Nasty, was shopping for a house. (Thank God, she was looking way across town.) Nasty encountered a real estate agent of highly questionable character, to say the least. This agent, Ms. Plastic, began by asking Nasty what type of home she was looking for, and how much she wished to spend. Nasty responded that she was seeking a small home with a big yard and mature trees. She could spend between $65,000 and $75,000.

Ms. Plastic then took Nasty on a tour of totally unsuitable $75,000 homes, until Nasty was near despair. They visited the run-down slum shack, grossly overpriced. They went to the new subdivision home, with its postage-stamp yard, and trees the size of houseplants. They inspected the house by the not-so-abandoned railroad tracks. (I'm sure the agent knew the train schedule.) Finally, they stopped to see a house that Nasty might just be interested in. Here's how Ms. Plastic announced this final candidate: "Well, I do have this one other. It just came on the market; it hasn't even been listed yet. You know, I really think they've underpriced it." Nasty snapped it up, before someone else could. Only after she moved in did Nasty realize there were 15 or 20 similar homes for sale in the neighborhood, for prices between $60,000 and $75,000. (The agent favored this particular home because she was the "listing agent" for it. She thus received both the seller's and buyer's portions of the commission.)

- Several years ago, I received a phone call from a Houston stockbroker seeking to add me as a client. Coincidentally, I already held an account with the national firm she represented. The woman wasn't aware of the existing account because it was registered in Tucson, Arizona, where I had previously lived and worked. I had maintained the Tucson

"*You better grab it. I've got several interested parties.*"

account because I liked my broker there, nicknamed "The Brick" (for his bad jokes). I could call the Tucson office toll-free using an "800" number.

I explained this to the woman on the phone, but she replied, "You better open an account here in town. The company is planning to eliminate those 800 numbers soon." I decided to ignore her and take my chances. To this day I can still call The Brick toll-free.

• One recent spring, before some planned traveling, I was shopping for a large foam mat or small conventional mattress to use while camping. Ultimately, I found a six-foot piece of foam at a hardware store, but it took a lengthy search. One place I ventured into was a large warehouse-style furniture store. From the outside, it seemed a good place to check, but once I stepped in I realized I'd made a mistake. It was more elegant inside than out: fine bedroom sets spread to the (distant) back wall. Price tags were heavy with ink. Before I could escape, a salesman, impeccably dressed, with his nose in the air, came my way. "May I help you, suh?"

I explained what I was after, and he reacted as if I'd told him I had the plague. He stepped back, to indicate I was dismissed. He was trying to make me to feel inferior. The fact that I wanted to make only a small, inexpensive purchase meant I was a low-life. But I wasn't concerned with this schmuck's opinion; I said thanks for nothing and left.

• A good friend of mine, Jay Bressler, once sold life insurance. He did it for only a few months; he couldn't stand the sleazy aspects of the business. Jay relates this tale which provides some insight into the profession:

"I was on my way to a sales meeting in Phoenix. This guy from the office, Midge, and I decided to car pool. All the way up, Midge keeps trying to convince me of the value of whole life insurance. 'Jay,' he says, 'you've got to sell more whole life. It's good for you and it's good for the customer. Stop selling all this term.' So I said, 'But Midge, I think term is right for some of my customers. They need $100,000 or $200,000 in coverage now, and they can't afford whole life.' 'No, no, no!' Midge shouts. 'Term insurance is rented insurance. You want to buy, not rent.' So finally I asked him, 'Midge, do you own any whole life yourself?' He looked at me like I had two heads. 'F—- no. Are you crazy?'"

Many salesmen will say or do anything to make a sale. The five stories just recounted are five of the millions that could be told. A "good" salesman has an immense bag of tricks. No one can warn you specifically of everything a salesman might try. Keep in mind that they, like advertisers, are aware of the seven basic purchase motives. Realize they are willing to seize upon a person's anxieties and imperfections. Most of all, recognize that salesmen will try to take advantage of your good nature. Most human beings tend to trust, so salesmen lie. Most people are uncomfortable rejecting another person, so salesmen absolutely will not take a polite "no" for an answer. An obnoxious salesman doesn't deserve your courtesy. If you've said "no" once to a salesman and it's fallen on deaf ears, get rude. Slam the door, walk away, scream at the top of your lungs — whatever. You're entitled.

There are two tactics used regularly by salesmen that I will warn you about. One was illustrated in the story of Nasty and the real estate agent. Salesmen will often attempt to induce a "state of urgency" in their customers. This results in the customer signing on the dotted line quickly, before getting a chance to shop around, and before doing any hard thinking. If a deal is legitimate, it's a good deal for both buyer and seller. It therefore won't vanish overnight. Always shop around, and always "sleep on" any major purchase decision.

The other commonly used sales stunt is the offer of something for nothing — that deal you "just can't pass up." Face facts, there are no free lunches in this world. You get what you pay for. At least, you don't get *more* than what you pay for; it's possible you may get less.

A warning bell should ring in your head whenever:

1. you get the feeling you must move quickly to close a deal before the opportunity vanishes
2. you think you're getting the far better end of a deal — as if you're almost "stealing" from the seller

If you find yourself in either of these situations, chances are you're being played like a fish. Just walk (swim?) away, before the hook is set.

The key to dealing with salesmen is to always gather product information from unbiased sources. Do not trust salesmen to provide you with information — it gives them a perfect opportunity to manipulate you. Educate yourself by talking to friends, or by scanning impartial books, magazines, and newspaper articles. It's usually not hard to locate a person at work, or some friend of a friend, who knows about cars, stereos, houses, insurance, or any of the myriad items that salesmen push.

If you feel you absolutely must deal with salesmen to get certain questions answered, survey several. You may get lucky and encounter an authentic human being, or you may simply find you're better able to sort out the lies after you've heard from several sellers. Hoping for the latter is risky, however. In some businesses, all the salesmen use the same lines (like Midge and his "term insurance is rented insurance"). If you do embark on an "educational trip" to speak with salesmen, consider leaving your checkbook, credit cards, and most of your cash at home.

26

The Manipulators III: Employers

I have worked for approximately 10 different employers in my life, and I've been exposed secondhand, through the experiences of friends, to dozens more. I don't generally care for employers; I feel they're manipulative. The very largest private employers, the Fortune 500 companies, strike me as the worst; I believe the vast majority of these corporate giants manipulate deliberately and systematically, using clever techniques. Smaller companies are usually cruder and less effective in their attempts to control employees, and quite a few small companies actually seem to treat their workers with due respect.

Decades ago, labor in this country reduced or stopped outright employer abuse in mines, mills, and factories. Labor unions forced companies to change policies and convinced legislators to pass protective laws. In today's world of the

8-to-5 office worker, however, abuse of workers by employers continues almost unchecked. The reason abuse at the office continues is that it is difficult to document, more so than turn-of-the-century abuse in factories. In the office setting, nobody has their hand smashed in a poorly designed machine; instead, the abused office worker develops ulcers, or becomes so surly at home he alienates loved ones. Today's abuses are largely psychological; it is a person's spirit that gets damaged now. Fortunately, if you identify "burnout" as a threat and realize employers shove people toward it, you are on the way to escape.

Working for Others — A Raw Deal

Have you ever wondered why someone pays you good money to sit at a desk and plot data, or make phone calls, or write reports? The answer, in most cases, is simple: your employer expects to profit by your efforts. Your employer expects to generate more money from your work than he pays you in wages. As long as that is the case, he will continue to employ you. In fact, he'll probably hire others and increase his profits. But if business turns sour, the hiring will stop and the firing will start. In other words, the typical employer views employees as a commodity, like scrap steel or pork bellies.

So what's in it for you? Why should you accept circumstances in which you're being paid less than the worth of your output? For starters, in many professions it's not possible to operate on your own. A large organization is needed to conduct business. It would be difficult, for example, for a geologist operating alone to drill an oil well — it's too expensive and involved. Another reason to work for others is for experience; you often "learn the trade" by working a few years under another person.

All in all, it isn't a good deal to work for someone. The few positives of the situation are offset by a host of negatives. We've talked before (Chapter 2) about how an 8-to-5 job thieves your time. Recall the typical office worker's weekday time budget; it left almost zero free time. And as an 8-to-5 employee, you have almost no freedom of schedule: you work those same eight hours, Monday through Friday, week after week. If it's sunny Thursday-Friday, but rainy Saturday-Sunday, that's your tough luck.

Worse than the daily or weekly schedule is the yearly one. Most big employers grant a pathetic two weeks vacation per year to new employees. After you've slaved continuously for a decade or two, you may find this bumped to three or four weeks. Think about that: you're born with 52 weeks off per year. You go to work for a big company, and it's 50 for them, two for you. That makes your cut about four percent! How would you feel if the IRS let you keep four percent —that's four cents — of every dollar you earned? (Don't say this too loud; they might get ideas.) What if tonight, instead of eight hours sleep, you got four percent of eight hours, or 19 minutes?

In addition, there's the Halo Effect. Most full-time employees work so hard they're exhausted by the time they leave work. They go home and collapse into an easy chair (often with a drink). When I worked at Shackles Oil, I was near death by Friday evenings. Weekend trips? I could manage one every couple months. Other weekends I needed to vegetate. In looking back, I find it incredible I was able to get myself up at 6:00 a.m., 200 days a year for work, but rose that early for fishing trips or golf only two or three times a year.

Quite simply, most employers ask so much of your time *and* *energy* it's an outrage.

But these are the complaints of relatively sane, aware people, those with enough self-esteem to take only so much. How about those workaholics? Employers exploit workaholics criminally. I know, firsthand and secondhand, of literally scores of salaried professional employees who routinely work 60- to 70-hour weeks! I kid you not — there is nothing else in these people's lives but work. And most of them are clearly miserable. (That is, it's clear to all but them.) Their faces are haggard; their voices drag. These people need more than self-help. They need psychotherapy. Or bosses that give a damn.

Obviously, I despise manipulative employers. They ruin people's lives. Let's look at how they pull it off.

The Lure

I described above certain positive aspects of working for others. You do get paid, and you may gain valuable experience. Some people may even enjoy the work they do for their employers, though I have a tough time empathizing with anyone who would prefer work to time off. At any rate, the positive reasons people have for working for employers are few. Indeed, these reasons may be restricted to the three just mentioned — money, experience, and in some cases, a mild enjoyment.

There are numerous negative reasons people work for others. Four stand out:

1. Some people feel the need to belong to a group. They need to be "accepted" by others.

2. Many people "need to be needed." They want other human beings to find them useful.
3. Some people desire authority in their lives. They want to follow, not lead or be independent.
4. People usually adhere to tradition, and tradition has it a person should work in a large organization and build a career.

In my opinion, these "reasons" reflect human weakness. And manipulators can be counted on to exploit human weakness.

Nearly all human beings require "approval" to some degree. Reasons 1 and 2 above, the need to belong and the need to be useful, stem from this need for approval. People's opinions of themselves depend on how they believe other people view them. People want to be liked and admired; it's a key to feeling worthwhile. Some outside opinions (of "worth") are more important than others. It is very important to be liked by your spouse, by your parents, by your kids. It is also important to be liked by teachers and bosses. The opinion of Joe the barber may be secondary. Generally, it is the opinions of people who see you most that count the most. In particular, it is the opinions of people who see *into* you that count — and the boss definitely sees the real you in your work.

The less you need approval, the better off you are; needs double as vulnerabilities. If you need to belong, or need to contribute, there are options besides work. Look to your family and friends for approval, not to some modern-day robber baron or his underlings.

The desire for authority (Reason 3) is especially pathetic. I have very little respect for the "follower" personality. Followers are either (1) too lazy to think for themselves, or (2) so lacking in courage they refuse to act on their thoughts. It is a mistake to hand control of your life over to authority (authority that is in many cases self-proclaimed). Such a surrender will never improve your life, and it could easily harm it. Benevolent authority is rare; most people or groups that have power over you will use you.

Reason 4 is no better than 3. Blindly adhering to tradition is a serious error. If a career is what you want out of life, go for it. Just make sure that you, not "The Establishment," made the choice. I consider career-building highly overrated. To me, the bottom line in life is achieving happiness. I don't see many happy faces in corporate management, nor among the young professionals striving to join them. What I mostly see are physically and mentally exhausted people who have lost control of their lives.

The Trap

Once people are lured into working for others, their positions often evolve into traps. Needless to say, employers commonly encourage this evolution. Three trapping mechanisms predominate:

1. The need for approval becomes all-consuming.
2. The employer is transformed into an absolute authority.
3. Crazed spending (particularly on credit) makes employment a financial necessity.

Two or all three of these mechanisms may operate together.

It is not unusual for a person to tie their sense of self-esteem completely or almost completely to their job. This leads to a terrible vulnerability: if such a person was to get fired or laid off they would be totally devastated. As a result such persons are like puppets on strings; employers can (and do) manipulate them at will. Job dependency this severe is a psychological problem. Several books deal with this problem. One I'm familiar with is *Divorcing a Corporation* by Jacqueline Hornor Plumez (Villard Books, 1986).

The authority trap is the one that employers make the greatest effort to promote. A majority of employers, and almost all big companies, attempt to induce dependency. They set themselves up as the givers and takers of all things, as artificial parents. The foremost tactic used by employers is the provision of benefits over and above salary: dental and health insurance, life insurance, a company car. Their goal is to take care of you, to fulfill your needs so quitting would be unthinkable. By design, the trap worsens with age — benefits increase with longevity: vacation increases, stock plans commence. After a number of years, it becomes almost impossible to quit. In this fashion, companies retain their valuable veteran employees. (Escalating benefits serve another purpose: there's always a new carrot dangling a year or two in front of an employee's nose.)

In many respects, employers treat employees like children, apparently in the hope they'll believe it. Employers have assorted petty rules — dress codes, schedules, "no dating of co-workers" policies. They have "discipline" procedures and demeaning employee evaluations akin to grade-school report cards.

Employers want very badly for you to forget one basic truth: a job is a simple exchange — an exchange of some amount of your services for some amount of the employer's money. You furnish a product, or perform a task, or provide a certain number of hours of labor, and the employer pays you a specified amount of cash. It's that simple. Employers like to put employees on salary, instead of hourly wage, so the employees will forget this truth. They can then work the employees more than eight hours a day, or more than 40 hours a week. Do not regard your employer as a master. Do not crown your employer next in a line of authority figures in your life (after your parents and your teachers). Retain your independence, your pride, your dignity, your spirit.

The last trap for discussion is the financial trap. But, in fact, we've discussed the financial trap throughout this book. Rampant spending will not improve a lousy existence; ultimately, it will make a lousy existence worse. Don't live paycheck to paycheck — your boss will own you. Build a Personal Treasury and lessen your dependence on work. Make firing a toothless threat.

27

The Manipulators IV: The Government

The United States government uses its laws to both force and influence the behavior of its citizens. I say "force and influence" because they use two types of laws to affect ordinary citizens. There are conventional laws, enforced by police, and there are tax laws, "enforced" by the IRS. (There are also laws that primarily affect businesses. Many of these are enforced by regulatory agencies with power to grant or revoke licenses.)

Conventional laws can be thought of as "do this or go to jail" laws. Tax laws can be thought of as "do this or pay taxes" laws. There's not much you can do if you don't like a law of the first type. You have to obey it; there's a gun to your head. Laws of the second type can be rejected; these laws are attempts at manipulation.

The Citizen Ideal

The U.S. government would like you to conduct your life as follows:

* take on a dependent spouse
* raise several children
* purchase and maintain a home
* buy, buy, buy, especially on credit

In short, the government would like you to follow The Standard Path.

There is logic behind the government's desires. Uncle Sam has reason to like the family unit, and to like "progress" (i.e., business activity). Large families represent more citizens, and citizens are a resource for government. They can be taxed; they can be drafted into the army. Increased business activity results in a more asset-rich country, and thus in a greater flow of tax dollars into government coffers. The government is just looking out for itself when it encourages you to be traditional.

This paints the U.S. government as a faceless entity, of course, which I think is fair. The government has evolved in the last two centuries into a juggernaut beyond the control of individuals. Even so, the politicians and the powers behind the politicians — those whose campaign contributions have placed the politicians in office — favor the status quo (tradition). They've made their life's fortunes off it.

If you don't believe the government is out to manipulate you, haul out your last year's tax materials, including the instruction booklet and tax table. Let's take a look. For a given adjusted gross income, someone "married, filing jointly" (the usual filing status for someone carrying a dependent spouse) experiences the lowest tax bill. Single persons pay much more, and anyone "married, filing separately" (a filing status used in some instances by married men and women whose partners work) really gets stung. As an example, let's compare tax bills for singles and married people with adjusted gross incomes of $44,000 in 1995, who claimed the standard deduction (i.e., who didn't itemize deductions):

	Married, filing jointly	Single	Married, filing separately
Adjusted Gross Income	$ 44,000	$ 44,000	$ 44,000
Standard Deduction	$ 6,550	$ 3,900	$ 3,275
Exemptions	$ 5,000	$ 2,500	$ 2,500
Taxable Income	$ 32,450	$ 37,600	$ 38,225
Tax	$ 4,871	$ 7,500	$ 8,168

Clearly, stay-at-home spouses are encouraged. Children are encouraged too: each dependent child is an additional exemption ($2,500 off taxable income in 1995). A batch of kids can be worth a grand or two off an annual tax bill.

Tax laws encourage home ownership by allowing loan interest and property taxes to be deducted. This can result in a tax savings of several thousand dollars per year. There is also a one-time capital gains tax exemption allowed for persons 55 years or older who opt to sell their home. This exemption eliminates (or reduces) the tax bill for individuals or couples who downsize their principal residence in their later years.

Tax laws discourage saving and, in effect, encourage spending. Investment income — interest on bank accounts, gains on stocks, gold, etc. — is taxed. You can't win: inflation cuts into your savings; earnings intended to offset inflation are clobbered by taxes (thanks to Uncle Sam on both counts). Incredibly, the purchase of toys and household items on credit was directly encouraged by the government for many years. Until 1990 consumer loan interest was fully deductible.

Be Yourself

It's nice to pay less in taxes, but in this, as in any situation, you need to view the total picture. If saving a few hundred or a few thousand dollars means complicating your life, it's not worth it. Don't let tax laws influence you to take major steps like acquiring dependents or buying a home. If you do elect to take on dependents and/or buy a home, your decisions should be based on legitimate personal desires. Don't let the government prod you down The Standard Path.

28

The Old Man
at the Campground

The Blue Ridge Parkway of North Carolina-Virginia is a breathtakingly scenic two-lane highway that winds for 469 miles through the southern Appalachian Mountains. It's a road with no stop signs, traffic lights, or billboards its entire length. The southern Appalachians are known for their classic fall colors and for the bright blooming azaleas and rhododendrons of late spring.

In May 1986 I was cruising this highway on my way to Washington, D.C., to meet a friend and tour the Smithsonian. The last days at Shackles Oil were four weeks past, and I was finally unwinding. For the first time in months I was truly enjoying life. I'd been able to hack my way to the end at Shackles by concentrating on the money I was making. Ultimately, I had taken to pinning photocopy blow-ups of $50 and $20 bills to my bulletin board. Two of the giant fifties and two of the giant twenties represented my proceeds per work day. I had calculated that each day I tolerated Shackles, I would earn approximately four days of future freedom and traveling.

On my third day driving the Parkway, late on a drizzly but nonetheless lovely afternoon, I pulled in for the evening at a nearly empty campground. A certain camaraderie exists among campers, especially when it's a bit off-season, and I soon had a visitor from one of the other campsites. A kindly old man, age 65 or 70, ambled over and struck up a conversation. It was a rather one-sided conversation (his), but I didn't mind — he was quite entertaining. To my surprise and pleasure, the talk strayed from the usual discussions of weather and scenery. Without any prompting from me, the old fellow began discussing the Leisure Life! A few of his choicer quotes:

"It's good to see a young person like you taking it easy and enjoying life. I should have retired much sooner than I did."

"You know, it really doesn't take much to live on."

Concerning his days of working at a country club:

"Those people were the unhappiest people I ever knew. All they cared about was who had the most money."

The happiest people, in his view?

". . . the campers. No doubt about it, the campers. Most of all, the tenters."

Pretty savvy fellow, don't you think? Amazingly, you wouldn't have thought so had you met him 10 years earlier. Ten years before, "The Old Man at the Campground" was just another working stiff, busting his butt, hardly knowing why. A bout with cancer had awakened him. (He'd nearly become a stiff of another sort.) The Old Man confessed: "There I was in my hospital bed, looking back at my life, filled with regret." Fortunately, the old fellow survived (sans one kidney) and received a few additional years to set things right. He and his wife sold most of their belongings, purchased an RV, and took to the road to see the country. The Parkway was their favorite spot; they spent three to four months of each year there.

As I continued my summer's travels I met a few other seniors who echoed the sentiments of The Old Man at the Campground. Old folks seem almost invariably to possess a remarkable understanding of the ways of the world. (There's no substitute for experience, I suppose.) Unfortunately, the elderly have only a few good years left in which to apply their knowledge. It's too bad people don't catch on sooner. ("Youth is wasted on the young.")

There's a trick you can employ for making big decisions. Ask yourself, "How will I view this decision years from now — whether 'yea' or 'nay' — upon looking back?" In other words, how will you view it when the actual emotions and pressures of the moment are forgotten? My guess is, in hindsight, most people will wish they'd "gone for it." They'll wish they'd said to hell with people's expectations, with fear of risk, and opted for a positive, exciting change in their lives.

Enjoy your 20s, 30s, and 40s, as well as your late 60s. "Go for it" — now. Remember, the best thing you can do with your money, with the fruits of your labor, is buy your freedom. Be frugal with your money in other facets of life, and you'll be free to get the maximum out of life.

I'll leave you with a joke. I don't remember where I heard it. My thanks to the author.

An old woman lay dying in a rest home, her dearest lifelong friend at her side. "I'm slipping away now, Emma. Be strong without me." Her words came slowly, between shallow breaths.

"I'll miss you, Mabel. But I'll be joining you soon enough, I suppose."

Mabel, now on nearly her last breath: "I've had a good life, Emma, I truly have — though I do have one regret."

Emma leaned closer to her friend, taking her hand. "What's that, dear? What is it that you regret?"

Mabel: "I wish . . . I wish I'd spent more time at the office."

Index

401(k) Plan, 63, 144-146

American Dream, 93-94, 121, 163
apartments, 128-129

Betty, Yuppie acquaintance, 39-40
Big E, The, credit card user, 47-48
Blue Ridge Parkway, 185
Bressler, Jay, friend who sold insurance, 169-170
Brick, The, stockbroker, 169

canoe incident, 98-100
Caveman Analogy, 58
Chumleys, archetypal consumers, 44-45
Consequence Costs, 50, 83-84, 86-87, 89, 93, 95-96, 122, 150
Consumer Price Index, 138-139
Convenience Purchases, 52, 67, 73-74, 150, 158
cost of living, 137-141
Cost-per-Use, 69-70, 73, 96
cottage at Petoskey, 96-98
Couples Syndrome, 118
coupons, 59
credit/credit cards, 43-48, 150

Dad, 96-98
Dan, friend in Houston, 86, 122-123, 133
Darwin, Charles/Darwinian Analogy, 134-136
Dejunking, 108, 113-119, 151
dependents, 90-93, 150-151, 152-153, 182-183
Divorcing a Corporation, by Jacqueline Hornor Plumez, 179

early retirement, 5, 29-32
Ego Acquisitions, 92
Ego Purchases, 52-53, 75-80, 150, 159
Elaine, spoiled sister, 115
Emma and Mabel, joke, 188
employers, 156, 173-180

Famous Visit to the Closet, The, 7-8
Four Cornerstones, 5-6, 132
Free Time Lost, 69

gold, 63
Golden Rule of Dejunking, 118
government, 156, 181-184
Guilt Acquisitions, 92
Guilt Purchases, 53, 75, 81, 150, 159
Guilt Time Expenditures, 101-104

Halo Effect, 13, 175-176
hobbies run amok, 70-72
home ownership, 93, 121-130,
150, 151-152, 183
homebodies, 123-125

Indentured International Oil,
former workplace, 7, 135
Individual Retirement Accounts
(IRAs), 63, 144-146
insurance, 64-66
Investment Purchases, 51-52,
61-64, 158

jadedness, 79

Koblenz, Dave, semiretired
friend, 37-39, 68

J. K. Lasser's Your Income Tax,
Macmillan, 147
Law of Possessions, 111-112
Leisure Life, 8-9, 12, 93,
149-153, 163, 186
Leisure, Lucell, IRA contributor,
145-146
LeMoine, Grant and Darth,
early-retired couple, 31-32, 68
lists, 108-109

Madison Avenue, 156-163
Manipulators, 156
McGee, Travis, Lifestyle, 36
Midge, insurance agent, 170
Mike, friend at Shackles Oil,
76-77
Milhous, Herbert Balfour,
$2.8 million winner, 1
Minimalism/Minimalists,
131-136, 137-138, 139-140,
143, 153

Mom, 114-115
Money Dynamics, by Venita
VanCaspel, 62
Money-for-Time Exchange Rate,
14, 59, 73
Money magazine, 62
Murphy's Law, 17-18

Nasty, former girlfriend, 98-100,
105-106, 122, 167
Need Purchases, 51, 57-61, 158
Need Time Expenditures, 102

Old Man at the Campground,
The, 185-187
organizing, 105-109

Parsons, Bo, Shackles Oil
employee, 3-4
Personal Treasury, 22-27, 30-32,
62, 91, 112, 132, 135, 151
Plastic, Ms., real estate agent, 167
Pleasure Acquisitions, 92, 150
Pleasure Purchases, 52, 67-72,
150, 158
Pleasure Time Expenditures, 102
Profit, Mr. and Mrs., Houston
home buyers, 126-128
Purchase Costs, 50, 86-87
Purchase Types, 51-56, 157-158

Rand, Ayn, 7
renting, 95-100, 151-152
river-reservoir analogy, 22-25
Riverswill Condominium
Complex, 166

salesmen, 156, 165-172
Save-to-Earn Ratio, 39-40
semiretirement, 5, 35-40
sentimentality, excessive, 114-115

Shackles Oil, former workplace,
  3-4, 8-9, 76-77, 185
shopping, 72
Simmerman, Quaid, friend in
  Arizona, 113
Social Security, 33
Standard Path, The, 93-94, 182

taxes/tax laws, 121-122, 139-140,
  143-147, 181-184
Tieback Principle, 85-86
Time Stealers, 101-104, 150
Tom, co-worker in Alaska, 41
Total Cost, 84, 86, 89, 95
Tradition Acquisitions, 91, 92
Tradition Purchases, 53, 75, 80-81,
  93, 150, 159
Tradition Time Expenditures,
  101-103
traps, 149, 152, 178-180

Urge to Possess, 79
urgency, state of, 170-171

Van Man, UCSD student, 133

weekday time budget, 13
Work Time Required, 69
Yuppie, Ms., 39-40

Give the gift of leisure!

Work Less and Play More **is the perfect tonic for your overworked, stressed-out spouse, friend, or child! Give your loved ones the gift of free time!**

Additional copies can be obtained at your local bookstore, or ordered directly from the publisher.

___ copies of *Work Less and Play More* @ $14.00 _____

Calif. residents only: **Sales Tax** @ $1.02 per book _____

Shipping $2.00

Total _____

Ship to:

Name: _____

Address: _____

_____

_____

Make checks payable to:

Kimberlite Publishing
P.O. Box 6334
Ventura, CA 93006